CLASSIC *f*M

50 MOMENTS THAT ROCKED THE CLASSICAL MUSIC WORLD

CLASSIC *f*M

50 MOMENTS THAT ROCKED THE CLASSICAL MUSIC WORLD

DARREN HENLEY AND SAM JACKSON

First published 2014
by Elliott and Thompson Limited
27 John Street
London WC1N 2BX
www.eandtbooks.com

ISBN: 978-1-90873-972-8

9 8 7 6 5 4 3 2 1

A CIP catalogue record for this book is available from the
British Library.

Cover design by davidwardle.co.uk

Typeset by Marie Doherty
Printed in the UK by TJ International

CONTENTS

CONTENTS

INTRODUCTION

This is one of those books that might cause arguments. Not the sort of argument that results in slammed doors, long-term sulks and all-round falling out, but rather the sort of argument that you might have with a close friend over a pint in the pub or while sipping a tall skinny wet latte in Starbucks. It will probably spark more of what you'd think of as an 'informed discussion' than an out-and-out row. You see, it's quite possible that we have set ourselves up for a bit of a fall with the whole concept of this book. Here we are writing the introduction and already we realise that we could be pilloried both for what we choose to include and because of what we choose to leave out.

If the truth be told, the idea of identifying 50 moments that have rocked the classical music world is a wholly subjective exercise. If you were sitting an exam and were asked to 'List the top 50 biggest changes in the development of classical music', there would be no definitive right and wrong answers, rather a set of differing points of view. This is the sort of book that critics love to review in the Sunday papers, because they can take issue with the central proposition and then give example after example of things that the author should have written. So, right at the start, we hold our hands up and admit the subjectivity of the book. It's partisan, and for that we are unapologetic. We realise it is unlikely that we have published a definitive list and that there could ever be complete consensus on how that list might look.

One of the great things about classical music is that it's a voyage of personal discovery. Even though Classic FM has been broadcasting the world's greatest music for more than two decades, every day we discover new classical works, exciting young artists and fresh recordings that cast old favourites in a completely new light. So, it's quite possible that if we had written this book ten years ago, or we were to sit down and write it all over again in ten years' time, then we might well arrive at a completely different set of 50 moments.

It's true to say that some of the moments we have chosen might unite pretty much all musicologists in agreement because there is a sense that they are universally regarded as being important factors in the way that music has developed; but other entries in our top 50 choices could bring some classical music experts out in hives. Equally, one or two musical historians will be very cross that their particular musical passions might seemingly have been overlooked altogether.

Those people who earn a living from composing and performing music right now might well take a different view again from those with a more historical perspective, possibly regarding the key points of substantial change in classical music's development as centring around their particular musical instrument or type of composition.

And then there's another group: those people who haven't studied classical music and don't work in the classical music industry, but nonetheless have built up a good working knowledge of the genre. They know what they like and might be surprised to find that there is less of a reflection of their own personal tastes in this book than they would perhaps like to see.

When you add in that people also tend to regard classical music slightly differently depending on where in the world they come from and which aspects of the genre they have been exposed to during their formative years, then our job is even further complicated.

We believe that each one of these groups is absolutely right in its view of the important bits of classical music – even though they all have slightly differing opinions of exactly what these important bits actually are. At the same time, we're more than happy to defend our own choices over the following pages.

So, let's be clear at the start. We have chosen these 50 moments after a huge amount of debate between ourselves. At first, we wondered whether we should include many more examples, but after hours of discussions (some of them over a pint in the pub, but more often while sipping one of countless tall skinny wet lattes in Starbucks) we eventually arrived at these 50 particular moments.

What were the criteria that we used? Well, as with all of our Classic FM books, we have rooted ourselves in the world of Classic FM itself and used this as the starting point for our deliberations. Since we first began broadcasting back in 1992, we have crystallised a very clear idea of what music our listeners want to hear and also what they would rather we didn't broadcast. Much of this information has been gleaned through extensive research among those people who already tune in to Classic FM on a regular basis as well as among those who are potential future listeners to the station.

We know that there is a great thirst for knowledge among the millions of people who listen to Classic FM across the UK each week. So, this book should very much be seen as a companion to two of our previous books: *The Classic FM Hall of Fame* and *Everything You Ever Wanted To Know About Classical Music . . . But Were Too Afraid To Ask*. The first of these books was an exploration of the top 300 most popular classical works, as voted in our annual listeners' poll, while the latter was an introduction to the whole gamut of classical music. We didn't just attempt to demystify the composers, eras and general musical terminology, but also to lift the lid on attending live concerts and building a collection of recordings for those people starting to find out about classical music for the very first time. If you have already enjoyed reading these two books, you might well see this new addition to your bookshelves as a natural next step along your journey of classical music discovery, as it allows us to pause along the way and delve into those major moments in more detail than we have done previously.

We are unequivocal in our belief that classical music can – and should – be enjoyed by everyone, no matter who they are or where they come from. So, it is inevitable that our own personal choices of the 50 moments that rocked the classical music world will centre on those events that have tended to have a democratising and proselytising effect. For us, each one of the 50 moments that we have chosen marks an important turning point in classical music's history. Usually, it consists of a radical departure from what had previously been seen as the norm. This change could have come from within the music itself, from the composers or performers, or it could be as a result of external forces, such as a particular technological advance or a new invention.

It's worth noting at this stage that although we talk throughout the book about particular 'moments' in classical music history, it would be fair to say that many of these 'moments' are hard to pin down. For example, there wasn't a particular day in a particular month in a particular year when every composer woke up in the morning and suddenly decided that polyphonic music was the order of the day. Instead, this was a culmination of years of musical development and the growth of a particular sound and style as different composers wrote music that added to the music of the time. But, nonetheless, the introduction of polyphonic music remains a momentous occasion in the overall story of classical music – and so we have chosen to include it here.

We hope that you agree with all 50 of our choices of the moments that rocked the classical music world, but we're sure you'll feel that some of your own personal favourites are missing. We would love to hear what you think – you can let us know by going to our website and filling in the online form at www.ClassicFM.com/50moments. Perhaps we will very quickly end up with enough of your ideas to fill the pages of a second volume. In the meantime, happy reading!

BANGING AND BLOWING: THE FIRST MUSICAL INSTRUMENTS

I n the mid-1850s, ancient human remains were discovered in the Neander Valley in Germany, providing evidence of some of the oldest human life known to date. The skeletons of people – soon nicknamed 'Neanderthals' after the place in which they were found – have provided a fascinating insight into life as far back as 100,000 years ago. Some of the more recent Neanderthal remains to have been uncovered demonstrate how music has been central to human existence for a great many centuries.

In 1995, Neanderthal skeletons were discovered at Divje Babe in Slovenia. Believe it or not, the leg bone of a young cave bear provided one of the most fascinating insights into the importance of music in the lives of our ancestors. The bone in question had clearly been broken at both ends and contained a series of adjacent separate holes. In other words, it could well have been a very early form of flute. Soon after its discovery, though, a debate raged among scholars as to whether this really was the world's oldest musical instrument, or whether it was, in fact, just a bone with a few bite marks in it. The debate has continued for many years, with a number of archaeological experts absolutely certain that the object is indeed a flute. If that is the case, then it provides proof that humankind has been making its own musical instruments for around 50,000 years or more.

Whether or not the so-called 'Neanderthal Flute' is indeed bona fide (if you'll excuse the pun), it's clear that many musical instruments have been around for thousands of years. The flute was definitely one of the earliest ones: even if the discovery in Slovenia was nothing more than an animal's leg bone, we know for sure that in *c.* 5000 BC, people in India were making primitive flutes out of wood. They even carved some of them into the shape of animals or birds. But the discovery at Divje Babe was an important moment in the history of classical music, because it encouraged people to question exactly when these instruments first made their imprint on history.

We should emphasise that it's impossible to pinpoint the exact moment of any early instrument's 'invention'. Very early humans probably knew a thing or two about percussion, even if they didn't yet have drums to hit or sticks with which to beat. And most of the instruments we hear today evolved over time, rather than being the brainchild of one particular man or woman. Nevertheless, the arrival of one instrument on the scene arguably changed the course of classical music more than any other. Prior to the 18th century, 'piano' was just an Italian word, meaning 'softly' or 'quietly'. But between 1700 and 1720, 'piano' took on a new sense, referring to the instrument that today transcends classical music, pop and rock to be one of the most famous inventions in world history. And, on this occasion, it *is* justified to refer to it as an invention.

Bartolomeo Cristofori worked for Prince Ferdinando de' Medici in Florence, where his role was to look after the royal court's instrument collection. He evidently had a little spare time, though, because when he wasn't tending to Prince Ferdinando's harpsichords he was able to invent an entirely new keyboard instrument, which would go on to change classical music for ever. In 1700, Cristofori created the first ever piano – which, crucially, had hammers and dampers, enabling the player to alter the volume of the sound each key made, something that had never before been possible. One of the earliest documents to describe this new instrument was written in 1711, by the journalist and poet Scipione Maffei. He referred to it as a 'gravicembalo col piano, e forte' – which translates as 'a harpsichord with soft and loud'. Hence the instrument eventually gaining the full name of 'pianoforte', (meaning 'soft loud'), which is commonly shortened to 'piano'.

Given its popularity across the world today, it seems remarkable that the piano was something of a slow-burner in early 18th-century Italy. You might be forgiven for presuming that this major new invention became the must-have instrument for any musical family or royal court, but it actually took quite some time for people to realise the significance of Cristofori's creation. Within a few decades, though, the piano's appeal had spread far and wide. In the Classical era, composers such as Mozart and Haydn wrote reams of music for the instrument, and it was often the case that famous composers were equally well known for their prowess as piano soloists.

The piano is unique in having a social history that runs alongside its musical history. By the end of the 19th century, it had become as common in aspirational middle-class households as fine bone china and a copy of *The Times* newspaper, whereas around the time of its invention, it was a rare and unusual instrument, which therefore cost a vast sum of money and was well out of the reach of the average person. It has become one of the most all-embracing of instruments: the piano is equally at home in a local pub as it is on the stage of London's Royal Festival Hall. Without doubt, Bartolomeo Cristofori's clever keyboard invention in 1700 was a moment that would go on to rock the classical music world – and the wider world, too.

SING A SONG OF CHRISTMAS: THE DEVELOPMENT OF THE CAROL

Many of the 50 moments described over the coming pages are, by definition, very easy to pinpoint: they focus on a precise date in history, when something seismic happened in the classical music world. Others, by contrast, are less simple to whittle down to a single moment, despite the fact that their impact was just as significant, if not more so.

In the case of the first Christmas carol, there's considerable debate as to when people started singing songs about the birth of Jesus. For Christians, the Gospel of Saint Luke provides the answer in Chapter 2, with angels singing on the night of Jesus's birth: 'Suddenly a great company of the heavenly host appeared with the angel, praising God and saying, "Glory to God in the highest heaven, and on earth peace to those on whom his favour rests"' (New International Version).

However, there is an argument that carols in fact predate Jesus's birth. The original meaning of the word 'carol' was 'to dance around something'. In the case of the early pagans, that 'something' would be a stone circle marking the position of the sun at the winter solstice. Whichever moment carols first started to be sung, it's clear that they have played a central role in the musical life of cultures across the world for thousands of years.

When it comes to the Christmas carols we know and love today, one of the oldest at the popular end of the repertoire is 'O Come, O Come Emmanuel' – or, to give it its original Latin title, 'Veni, Veni, Emmanuel'. Composed as a 12th-century chant, it wasn't translated into English until the 1850s, at which point its popularity spread in this country and beyond. But there are many examples of the Christmas carol tradition before this: barely a century after the death of Jesus, the then Bishop of Rome apparently encouraged priests to sing songs about Christmas. It wasn't until the 13th century, though, that ordinary people were invited into the world of carolling.

Francis of Assisi, who has since been dubbed 'The Father of Carolling', didn't think it right that the only people who sang Christmas carols were priests. He wanted everyday Catholics to participate in this joyful act – which, to be honest, had been a rather solemn affair when left solely in the hands of the priests. As he looked back on that ancient scripture about the very first Christmas, Francis wanted to communicate something of the joy of the season, with ordinary people singing out songs of hope and encouragement. This also inspired his creation of the world's first public nativity scene, at a church in Italy in 1223 – again, something that would bring the Christian message to the masses rather than keeping it exclusively to church officials. It was at this point that, as far as we're able to, we can pinpoint a precise moment when the classical music world was rocked – for, in 1223, Francis of Assisi composed the song *'Psalmus in Nativitate'*. Containing accessible music and Latin words, this was probably the first dedicated Christmas carol.

Francis of Assisi was passionate about spreading the word about Christianity. To quote his biographer, the 13th-century writer Thomas of Celano, 'The Child Jesus was forgotten by the hearts of many. But with the grace of God He was resurrected again and recalled to loving memory in those hearts through His servant, the Blessed Francis.' All his carols were written in Latin, but the tradition soon spread from Italy to other parts of Europe – most notably, France and Spain. The first song written in England with the express purpose of being a carol dates from the turn of the 15th century, and before long, many fine composers were writing music for the season.

It was soon commonplace for carols to be sung among groups of people – in homes, in streets, wherever members of the public gathered together. Francis of Assisi was a real democratiser of this music, taking it beyond the four walls of the church and encouraging ordinary people to experience carols for themselves. You yourself might have gathered with some of your neighbours at Christmas time, going from door to door singing carols together; this tradition is actually centuries old, and is one of the consequences of St Francis's desire to spread the Christmas message to as many people as possible.

Perhaps surprisingly, there are occasions throughout history when carols have caused controversy. *'O Come, All Ye*

Faithful', for example, might not be all it seems – certainly not if some research published by a Durham-based academic in 2008 is to be believed. Professor Bennett Zon, Head of Music at Durham University, told the *Daily Telegraph* that the original Latin version of the carol, *Adeste Fideles*, might have had a hidden meaning. 'There is far more to this beloved song than meets the eye,' he said. 'Fideles is Faithful Catholic Jacobites . . . The meaning of the Christmas carol is clear: "Come and Behold Him, Born the King of Angels" really means, "Come and Behold Him, Born the King of the English" – Bonnie Prince Charlie!'

And that's not all: in the Victorian era, there were concerns that the relatively modern carol *'While Shepherds Watched Their Flocks by Night'* was too secular in its approach, with simple words that lacked the beauty (and, therefore, holiness) of other sacred songs.

In the last couple of centuries, the tradition of Christmas carolling has developed still further. In many ways, it has come full circle: non-religious carols existed before the birth of Christ, and in the last 200 years lots of secular carols have been composed – from *'Deck the Halls with Boughs of Holly'* to *'O Tannenbaum'*, and *'Jingle Bells'* to *'The Twelve Days of Christmas'*. All of these songs owe a debt of gratitude to Francis of Assisi – because, without him, the tradition of singing music together at Christmas time might never have developed in such an all-embracing way.

GETTING IT WRITTEN DOWN: THE INTRODUCTION OF MUSICAL NOTATION

Just like any other form of communication, music is a language. Through it, we can share something powerful that speaks to us very deeply – and the method that enables this to happen is one of the most significant developments in the history of all music.

Whether or not you play an instrument, the chances are that you already have at least a basic understanding of what written-down music looks like. Most commonly, those five horizontal lines (the stave); the hashtag-style sharp and the flat that looks like a wonky letter 'b'; and the variously decorated notes, all of which give the performer an idea of what they should be playing and how it should sound. And, just as the development of the written word was pivotal to the spread of language, so the invention of notation was a true line-in-the-sand moment in the musical world.

We can be almost certain that music of some form or another has been part of life since the dawn of time. From birdsong right the way through to that innate human tendency to whistle a tune, it's likely that music has been in existence for as long as humanity. Writing in the *Musical Times and Singing Class Circular* way back in 1866, one Henry C. Lunn commented, 'I do not intend to frighten my readers by attempting to discover the origin of music. We have a right to believe it commenced with the existence of man upon the earth.' But when it comes to notation, as far as we're able to pinpoint a precise moment in history, we have to turn our attention to the 1st century AD – and to a piece of music known as the *Seikilos Epitaph*.

This was, quite simply, a song of its day, with both the music and the Greek lyrics notated on a piece of stone. It was discovered in the late 19th century, and for the very first time, human beings could begin to understand the point at which their forebears had first started to communicate music visually. It evidently took quite some time, though, before this primitive form of notation morphed into the traditional 'five lines with notes' approach with which we're so comfortable nowadays. And while we don't know who to credit for the *Seikilos Epitaph*, there's no doubt who was responsible for the style of music notation used across most of the world today.

Guido of Arezzo was an Italian monk, born just before the turn of the 10th century, and he goes down in history as one of classical music's most influential figures. Quite simply, his new approach laid the foundations for pretty much all the music composed after him. If you've ever wondered whom we have to thank for all those notes and dots on the pages of musical manuscript paper, you've found your man. Not only was Guido a monk, he was also a respected academic and invented the system of notation that we still use today. His real name was Guido Arentinus, with 'Arezzo' coming from the Italian region of the same name, where he lived out the end of his life. Guido was quite the innovator: in addition to coming up with the idea of musical notation, he also challenged the status quo in various monasteries where he was a monk. In his writings, Guido chronicled his attempts to make changes to some of the approaches to liturgical singing. These didn't always go down well with the powers that be, even leading to him being evicted from the monasteries where he lived.

Fast-forward on a few centuries, and the invention of the printing press enabled a much quicker dissemination of written music (see Moment No. 8), but we needed a system by which the notes could be written down long before this could happen. In the 21st century, notated music is perhaps the most widely understood written language in the world. Those minims, crotchets and quavers are comprehended on a very wide level by people of different races, backgrounds and beliefs. When he devised his own primitive form of notation some 2,000 years ago, Guido of Arezzo could not have begun to imagine the development of his ideas over the centuries that followed – but he would surely be rather proud of where that germ of an idea of his has led.

CHANGING THE TUNE: THE FIRST USE OF POLYPHONY

I t would be fair to presume that you, like us, have never flicked through the *Musica enchiriadis* from cover to cover. This 9th-century treatise contains the first record of 'polyphony' – a musical form, the invention of which was a major moment in history, laying the foundations not just for the likes of Bach and Beethoven but for many forms of jazz, pop and rock music, too.

Up until this point, the only known type of music was monophonic. In other words, it had just one, single melodic line, with not much else going on. With the advent of polyphony, music suddenly became rather interesting: two or more melodies could be heard simultaneously, meaning it was possible to add harmonies, embellishments and all sorts of other exciting new ideas to what we might nowadays simplistically call the 'tune'.

This new form of music was by no means 'discovered' in the 9th century, though; rather, it evolved and developed over the best part of six centuries, being widely used within musical circles only from the 1400s onwards. Much of this development took place in the 11th and 12th centuries – a really exciting time, when music, painting and other art forms were gaining new ground and changing at quite a rapid rate. Initially, polyphony manifested itself through chant. Voices would not just sing in unison; instead, one voice would sing a little higher or a little lower than the main melody. Fast-forward on to the end of the 12th century, and polyphony had become more florid. In Paris, the choir of Notre Dame Cathedral was singing an ornate form of music that was the brainchild of a composer by the name of Léonin, who put together the *Magnus liber organi* (the 'Great book of organum' – organum being a form of polyphony).

The 20th-century philosopher Karl Popper once described polyphony as 'possibly the most unprecedented, original, indeed miraculous achievement of our Western civilisation, not including science'. In fact, the secular nature of its development led to quite some controversy when members of the Catholic Church attempted to introduce polyphonic music to their sung worship. For Christians who had been used to a simple, solemn and uncluttered form of music, the idea of singing different lines, adding in harmonies and welcoming in a form most associated with those outside the Church, was deeply questionable. They also argued that this more intricate style of singing could risk the words becoming lost entirely. As sacred melodies became more layered, with added harmonies appearing around them, there was a fear that the texts being sung to those melodies might have ended up being an irrelevance – not something the Catholic Church wanted to see happening.

Heated debates about the supposedly inappropriate nature of polyphonic music reached their height in Europe in the 14th century. In 1322, Pope John XXII issued a papal bull forbidding its use in church, believing it to be an ungodly form of music. He wrote, 'There are certain disciples of the new school who, devoting all their attention to measuring time, apply themselves to the making of notes in a different fashion . . . They chop up the chant with notes of short values . . . pollute the melodies with descants and go as far as to muffle the upper voice in the vulgar tongue . . . Under this avalanche of notes, the chaste ascensions and discreet closes of the plainsong, by which the tones themselves are distinguished, become unrecognisable.'

Today, this level of paranoia about polyphonic music seems astonishing, but back then, this was a topic that exercised people very deeply. The Church was worried at the way in which secular music appeared to be taking hold over its own traditions of worship. The Pope was primarily concerned with a movement known as 'Ars Nova', which was based in France and which embodied everything the Church feared. Musicians allied with the movement would sometimes encourage people to take a sacred melody and sing a secular text over the top – the ultimate sullying of something holy, as far as Church authorities were concerned.

In 1342, a new pope, Clement VI, was installed at the Vatican, and he brought with him a change of attitude towards polyphony. Clement was himself a fan of this form of music: he didn't share his predecessor's fears, and polyphony was therefore free to take hold in the sacred space just as much as it had done in secular circles. Nevertheless, it's worth bearing in mind that, at this point in history, classical music as we know and love it today was still very much in its infancy. Johann Sebastian Bach would not be born for another 300 or so years, and the world would have to wait even longer before it was graced with the genius of Mozart and Beethoven.

The first real golden age of polyphonic music was not until the 16th century, and was arguably best embodied in England and Italy. The English composer Thomas Tallis is responsible for writing the most famous example of polyphony in the history of choral music. His motet 'Spem in Alium' was composed for 40 voices, all singing independent, interweaving lines that together create the most glorious wall of sound. In Italy, meanwhile, Giovanni Pierluigi da Palestrina was the greatest example of a master of polyphonic music: you have only to listen to his 'Stabat Mater' or the Missa Papae Marcelli to hear this for yourself.

The development of polyphony therefore had huge ramifications in the classical music world. It seems unfathomable for us now to imagine never being able to listen to a harmony, instead enjoying only a single line of plainchant rather than richly textured music. The introduction of polyphony is as important to other musical genres as it is to classical music. Put simply, a world without polyphonic music from the likes of Oscar Peterson, the Beach Boys and Elbow is just as hard to imagine.

5

THE CRUELLEST CUT: CASTRATI COME TO PROMINENCE

For two male authors, there's only one word than can fully encapsulate the enormity of this particular classical music moment: 'Ouch!' During this chapter, we shall explore just why the use of castrati was so important and how it came to become one of the most controversial aspects of Western music. We assume the concept of castration is one you're familiar enough with already (although we hope not through first-hand experience). If it's not, prepare to be disappointed, because we're not going to be exploring the finer details of this particular medical procedure.

In terms of pinpointing an exact moment when castrati became commonplace in the performance of classical music, we're going to plump for around 1550. Admittedly, there are records to show that castration was taking place in ancient times, as far back as 2500 BC; however, it wasn't until the 16th century that the practice became commonly associated with music. The sole musical advantage of castration is that it retains in an adult male the pure, pre-pubescent singing voice of his youth. The process has various physiological effects, too: among them, increased breath control and an extraordinary vocal range. Unsurprisingly, therefore, the beauty of the castrato voice was of immense appeal to certain composers, even if the means by which it had to be achieved was so unpleasant.

By the late 1550s, castrati were already regular fixtures in the choir at the Sistine Chapel, and over the next 20 years, they would come to be found in ensembles throughout Europe, particularly in Germany and France. The Vatican endorsed the process, as evidenced by the fact that, in 1589, the Pope arranged for castrati to be welcomed into the choir at St Peter's Basilica in Rome.

By the turn of the 16th century, it's fair to say that the use of castrati in choral singing was not just to be welcomed: it was to be expected. Various male soloists made a name for themselves as castrato singers: Loretto Vittori spent the best part of half a century as a soprano singer in Rome's papal chapel; and the Perugian singer Baldassare Ferri became famous throughout the whole of Europe, making a fortune out of his talents and dying a very rich man indeed.

You might well wonder why on earth the Church, in particular, needed castrati even in the 16th century. The answer to this question is simple: women were banned from taking part in any sacred service, so choirs had to be exclusively male. Consequently, the feminine qualities of the castrato voice were hugely appealing, given that they mimicked a woman's voice and tone without actually requiring the presence of a female in the choral ranks. Although the practice of castration did thankfully start to die away during the 18th century, castrati still formed a part of the Sistine Chapel choir as recently as 1903.

Castrati weren't just restricted to the Church, though. Their presence rocked the classical music world precisely because of their use in secular circles, too. Take, for example, Monteverdi's opera *Orfeo*, where castrati were put to very good use in a number of different roles. The craze for these singers continued unabated until the early 18th century when, at its height, it was reported that around 4,000 boys were being castrated every year, solely for musical purposes. As late as 1824, the Italian composer Giacomo Meyerbeer premiered his opera *The Crusader in Egypt*, containing the character of Armando, who could be sung only by a castrato.

Sadly, a disproportionate number of castrated boys came from poverty-stricken backgrounds. All too often, parents put their son forward as a candidate for castration in the hope that his ensuing success would bring home some kind of financial reward.

Ever since the emergence of castrati in the 16th century, their existence in the musical world has been accompanied by a fair amount of controversy. The not inconsiderable physical risks of the operation aside, castrati were also subjected to near-total humiliation and rejection in social circles. Their sexuality was questioned; they could never marry, and the abnormal changes to their bodies caused many to suffer from severe psychological distress. Several very senior members of the Catholic Church, including one pope, expressed their displeasure, too. As early as the 1740s, Pope Benedict XIV attempted to ban the practice but he was shouted down by those who feared it would diminish church attendance. These half-men, half-boys had become something of a curiosity for the Italian public, who would flock to churches far and wide to hear them in action.

The only castrato ever to have been recorded was Alessandro Moreschi – an Italian, unsurprisingly, who lived until 1922 and who was still singing publicly at the start of the 20th century. This youthful-looking man was known for being able to perform Caccini's *Ave Maria* with beautiful purity, at the age of 55.

For the best part of 350 years, castrati formed an important, if curious, role in the musical life of Italy. Although the practice never fully spread across Europe, it remained a highly controversial and influential musical oddity, which mainstream composers saw no harm in embracing. Thankfully, the combination of social unease, the gradual acceptance of female musicians, and the decision on the part of the Catholic Church consciously to distance itself from the practice, means that castration for musical purposes has now been consigned to the history books.

STRIKE UP THE BAND:
THE INVENTION OF THE SYMPHONY

C an anyone really be described as a 'great composer' if they have never written a symphony? This particular genre of classical music has been responsible for some of the most popular and revolutionary pieces ever composed – from Mozart's *'Jupiter'* through to Mahler's *'Resurrection'*, via Beethoven's *'Choral'* and Berlioz's *Symphonie fantastique*. When it comes to rocking the classical music world, the symphony has played a huge part in introducing entirely new sounds to an unsuspecting public, throughout the course of history. But how did it all begin?

The word 'symphony' translates as 'sounding together'. So, musically speaking, it relates to more than one instrument or voice being heard together at the same time. In that sense, there are examples of 'symphony' stretching back to the dawn of time – but in terms of how we define the symphony today, we want to home in on what was happening in the middle of the 18th century. It was then that the

word 'symphony' started to take on an entirely new meaning. Previously, it had been interchangeable with musical
forms such as 'overture' or 'sinfonia' – but from then on,
'symphony' would refer to a specific type of orchestral piece
made up of three or four movements.

The person we have to thank for the structure of the symphony as we know it today is the Austrian composer Joseph
Haydn. This man, known as the 'Father of the Symphony',
composed over a hundred of them during his life. Crucially,
though, he was also the trendsetter when it came to what
a modern symphony should sound like. In his early years
as a composer, Haydn was given the chance to experiment
with this new sound-world and in 1761 he wrote three very
fine early symphonies, all with nicknames: *No. 6* ('Le Matin'),
No. 7 ('Le Midi') and *No. 8* ('Le Soir'). The immense popularity of these three pieces in particular led to the spreading of
Haydn's fame across Europe: by 1781, he had become the
first composer to have his symphonies published in England.
A string of commissions for further symphonies followed,
including six from France – where, just as in England, Haydn
was being celebrated for this outstanding new music.

The development of the symphony within the Classical
period is indelibly linked with the invention of something
called 'sonata form'. There are whole books dedicated to this
particular topic and it would be fair to say that not all of
them are exactly gripping page-turners for even the most
inquisitive and dedicated classical music fan. But, essentially,
we reckon that all you need to keep in your mind is that
the expansive musical structure of sonata form enabled composers to break away from the 'binary' form of the Baroque

period, which had made the expression of ideas on a large scale quite tricky at times.

Although we can't name one exact date when the symphony burst onto the scene, it's likely that without Haydn we would not have seen this musical form develop at such a pace. Mozart, composing in the same Classical era as Haydn, wrote 41 symphonies. And, of the nine Beethoven composed, a great many were groundbreaking. Think of the Third, the 'Eroica', which heralded the arrival of the Romantic era of music (much more on this one in Moment No. 20); the Fifth, with those famous four opening notes; the bucolic Sixth, nicknamed the 'Pastoral'; or the mighty Ninth, known as the 'Choral' – which, for many listeners, sits at the summit of all symphonic music.

In the Romantic period, the symphony really came into its own. Bring to mind a famous composer from the 19th century and you can bet your bottom dollar he was probably known for his symphonies. Tchaikovsky used the form in the most remarkable of ways, from his fate-filled *Symphony No. 4* to the tragedy and pathos in his final *Symphony No. 6* (the 'Pathétique'). Fans of Rachmaninov, meanwhile, will argue that no one has composed a better heart-on-your-sleeve melody than the sweeping opening to the third movement of his *Symphony No. 2*. And Brahms, who waited until he was in his forties to write a symphony, saved many of his best ideas until last, with one critic dubbing his *Symphony No. 1* 'Beethoven's Tenth' – the highest praise the composer could have hoped for.

As the symphony developed, it created a musical genre in which boundaries could be pushed in remarkable ways.

One of the most exciting examples of this is Mahler's *Symphony No. 8* – nicknamed the '*Symphony of a Thousand*', although not by the composer himself. What Mahler *did* say, however, was that in writing this work he wanted to create 'a new symphonic universe'. He most certainly achieved this goal. The forces Mahler used were on a scale unlike any ever seen before: a huge orchestra, including four bassoons, two contra-bassoons, an enormous percussion section and an entirely separate trumpet ensemble. On top of that, he included an organ, some pianos, a few harps, two adult choirs, a children's choir and eight solo singers. Although the soundscapes of this mighty work are, on one level, a million miles away from an early Haydn symphony, it's logical to argue that without the Haydn, we wouldn't have had the Mahler.

History has witnessed symphonic extremes in the other direction, too. There are plenty of short symphonies in existence: Mozart's *Symphony No. 32*, for example, lasts for barely eight minutes. But what must surely rank as the shortest symphony ever composed dates from this century. In 2002, Michael Wolters's *Spring Symphony:The Joy of Life* was given its premiere performance at the Huddersfield Contemporary Music Festival. According to the composer, the piece was never actually intended to be performed. Instead, he describes it as 'conceptual rather than realistic', and it was only when urged by a friend to have the piece played in public that Wolters relented. The work is so fleeting that the composer attempted to get it recognised in the *Guinness Book of World Records* as the world's shortest symphony. It last for just 14 seconds – or as many as 16 seconds, if the performers are playing it a little on the slow side.

MAKING IT IN A MAN'S WORLD: HILDEGARD OF BINGEN

As you'll no doubt notice as you flick through the pages of this book, many of the moments we describe involve huge personalities, historic one-off events and, in some cases, a fair whiff of scandal. So how come a modest 12th-century nun is to be found here – and what did she do to change the course of musical history?

Before exploring the answer to these two questions, let's pause for a second or two and consider the following utterance, made by the playwright and author George Bernard Shaw. After attending a concert in London, he commented, 'When E. M. Smyth's heroically brassy overture to *Antony and Cleopatra* was finished, and the composer called to the platform, it was observed with stupefaction that all that tremendous noise had been made by a lady.' If the appearance of a woman as the composer was a novel idea in the 20th century, it could have been described as nothing less than revolutionary eight hundred years earlier.

Hildegard of Bingen lived during the Middle Ages and is recognised today by musical historians as being the first significant female composer. Even now, in the 21st century, men overwhelmingly dominate the world of classical music composition. And the levels of equality aren't much better when it comes to performing in some areas of classical music too. Take the Vienna Philharmonic Orchestra as an example. Unbelievably, it did not allow female members to join until as late as 1997. The vast majority of famous conductors are male, although the likes of the American Marin Alsop are blazing a trail for women on the podium. So, it's all the more remarkable that, eight centuries ago, Hildegard of Bingen, a female composer, theologian and mystic, was able to establish herself and to leave a musical legacy.

Hildegard was born in 1098 in the region of Alzey, which now forms part of modern-day Germany. The tenth child of relatively wealthy parents, she was marked out as being someone special from a very young age – so much so that, by the time she turned eight, her parents had decided that she must devote the rest of her life to a religious order. Bear in mind: such a decision would have had huge ramifications, not least because she would never be able to marry or to have children of her own. By the age of fourteen, Hildegard had professed her vows as a Benedictine nun, and was fully ensconced into the practices and disciplines of religious life.

Initially, it was Hildegard's spirituality, rather than her musical prowess, that ensured she was listened to by the public at large. Her reputation as a healer and prophet who could hear directly the word of God ensured that pretty much anything she produced would be taken notice of, whether in the form of spiritual pronouncements or musical compositions. Her output was prolific: in addition to a published book of song cycles and a musical play, she also wrote three books on theology and a further two on medicine. As she entered adulthood, Hildegard was all too aware that her status as a woman was in no way helpful when it came to her vocation as a composer. Unsurprisingly, despite her considerable natural ability, she downplayed her talents, conscious that she might well have been prohibited from writing music if she stood out too much. It wasn't until the year 1141, when Hildegard was in her early forties, that a professed vision from God led her to embrace her calling fully on every level.

In her excellent book, *Hildegard of Bingen: The Woman of Her Age* (published by Faber and Faber), the classical music writer Fiona Maddocks reports that Hildegard described the vision like this:

And behold! In the forty-third year of my earthly course as I was gazing with great fear and trembling attention at a heavenly vision, I saw a great splendour in which resounded a voice from Heaven, saying to me, 'O fragile human, ashes of ashes, and filth of filth! Say and write what you see and hear. But since you are timid in speaking, and simple in expounding, and untaught in writing, speak and write these things not by a human mouth, and not by the understanding of human invention, and not by the requirements of human composition, but as you see and hear them on high in the heavenly places in the wonders of God. Explain them in such a way that the hearer, receiving the words of his instructor, may expound them in those words, according to that will, vision and instruction. Thus, therefore, O human, speak these things that you see and hear. And write them not by yourself or any other human being, but by the will of Him Who knows, sees and disposes all things in the secrets of His mysteries.

This vision led to Hildegard becoming something of a local celebrity and a religious phenomenon. Pilgrims flocked to meet her, as news of her direct line to God spread far and wide. All the while, she remained a musician and composer, as part of her dedication to the spiritual life.

Hildegard continued to challenge authority. When she moved with eighteen fellow nuns to form a community in Rupertsberg in 1150, she pushed for nuns and monks to receive equal dowries (at that time, the monks were better remunerated). She also encouraged the nuns to dress differently: wearing their hair unbound, for example, adorned with beautiful tiaras. All this went hand in hand with her spirituality: Hildegard believed such attire brought glory to God because it emphasised the beauty of femininity.

In her day, Hildegard of Bingen was revolutionary: her advice was sought by popes and secular leaders; her message was heard by hundreds as she travelled as an itinerant preacher; and she was regarded as an important composer. Since then, there have been a great many fine female composers – from Clara Schumann and Fanny Mendelssohn in the 19th century through to Ethel Smyth and Amy Beach in the 20th. Although these women seem all too often to be airbrushed out of classical music history, with their contributions frequently ignored, this line of female composers threads right back to Hildegard of Bingen. And that really shouldn't be ignored.

SHARING THE MUSIC: THE INVENTION OF THE PRINTING PRESS

As we pointed out a little earlier, music has been part of human existence for many centuries. Long before it was possible to read this music as symbols on a sheet of paper, our ancestors were banging sticks, making melodies and experimenting with ideas of rhythm and pitch. But, from the 15th century onwards, thanks to the invention of the printing press, it became possible for music to be shared on a mass scale for the very first time – and this was to transform the lives and the fortunes of many great composers.

The era from the late 15th to the early 16th centuries was a hugely exciting time. This particular section of the Renaissance period included all sorts of developments in the worlds of art and culture, and the ability to print music was the result of a great deal of technological experiment and advancement. Some of this was evolutionary, having been developed over time; other aspects were completely new. Take, for example, the invention of moveable type, which made it possible for lines and staves to be set on the page – and for accurate printing to take place very rapidly. These developments were mirrored in other areas: literature became more readily accessible, and news and information could be spread far more quickly than ever before.

The person we have to thank for the invention of the printing press is a certain Johannes Gutenberg, who used one for the very first time in 1450. Before long, the printing press was being employed for musical purposes – and it had three distinct benefits. Firstly, this new system could ensure complete legibility: musical symbols were standardised, and musicians no longer had to decipher the individual handwriting of a particular composer or copyist. Secondly, the rather painstaking process of lining up all the notes and symbols would ultimately ensure the score was completely accurate before printing, with no need for any revisions afterwards. And, thirdly, once the process of creating the musical score was complete, it could be duplicated very quickly. This final development was perhaps the most exciting; previously, every single score would have to be copied out by hand, a process that could take months. Now, thanks to Gutenberg's exciting new invention, printed music could be spread across Europe relatively quickly.

The first piece of music ever to appear in a printed volume was in a compendium called the *Codex spalmorum* in 1457. In Britain, the Renaissance composers who benefited most from this new technology were Thomas Tallis and his pupil William Byrd. The monarch at the time, Elizabeth I, granted them a licence to print and publish their own music, which had two immediate outcomes: their compositions became far more widely known, and their income rocketed. The publishing of music was (and still can be) a fairly lucrative affair, and the ability these two composers had to disseminate their work had a sizeable impact on their fortunes. All of a sudden, Tallis, Byrd and other composers from across Europe could, for the first time, make an independent living from their works, without having to remain solely reliant on wealthy supporters and patrons. And the fact that they were able to print their music by royal appointment gave absolute legitimacy to this new approach.

It's worth pointing out that the arrival of the printing press did bring with it various challenges, too. The process of setting every note, symbol and stave, and ensuring they all printed correctly, was an incredibly tricky one. Workers would often not be paid if they made a mistake, and it took a great deal of time for people to become accustomed to the new-fangled equipment. Often, it was a case of 'two steps forward, one step back' as developments in technology were made, only for the people using the equipment to then struggle to operate it correctly. It was frequently the case that workers would enlist the help of a master printer, who would have the knowledge and experience to teach others how to use the printing press correctly.

For all that the printing press offered, it was a difficult piece of equipment – and there was a danger that if those operating it didn't know how to use it, it would become an unnecessarily costly affair. Although the printing press offered a far speedier way of copying musical parts compared to the former method of writing everything out by hand, it wasn't always easy to do. The actual printing process had a number of different layers to it: first, the lines of the stave would need to be carefully placed on the paper; then, the notes would need to be placed on top (with absolutely no margin of error allowed); and, after that, everything would have to be meticulously checked before additional copies of the music were made.

The development of the printing press was by no means done and dusted in the 1500s. Changes were made well into the 18th century, with new typefaces invented for use on the musical page and cleaner, clearer ways of printing music being developed. The creation of new fonts was of crucial importance, and there was a healthy rivalry between different companies: the London-based Caslon, for example, and a German firm called Breitkopf. Since the 18th century, the approach to printing music has continued to evolve. Nowadays, for example, some musical scores don't even reach the stage of being printed: plenty of musicians prefer to read notated music from the screen of an iPad, rather than carrying around dog-eared pieces of paper.

It's clear, though, that without the development of the printing press some five hundred years ago, the musical world would have been an infinitely poorer one. Classical music spread far and wide thanks to this wonderful new invention, and people simply would not have been able to learn, play, sing and study this music without it. Johannes Gutenberg's achievement was a mighty one, and all of us who love music should feel an enormous debt of gratitude towards him.

BY ROYAL APPOINTMENT: THE
MASTER OF THE KING'S MUSICK

Back in the 14th century, royal patronage in England was awarded only to a very select group of musicians, who were known by all and sundry as the 'King's Minstrels'. Back then, according to official records, Edward IV employed a total of thirteen minstrels, 'whereof some be trumpets, some with shalmes and small pypes'. Henry VIII, getting on for a century later, was well on his way to employing a full orchestra, consisting of '15 trumpets, 3 lutes, 3 rebecks, 3 tamborets, a harp, 2 viols, 9 sackbuts, a fife and 4 drumslades'.

Over time, the number of royal musicians steadily grew until, in 1626, a brand new position was invented: the Master of the King's (or, latterly, Queen's) Musick, with the extraneous letter 'k' remaining in place until the 20th century. With the exception of an eleven-year break from 1649, the position has been held continuously, and it has led to the creation of some very fine music over the last four centuries.

The first man to be appointed to the role (one that has

continued to be an exclusively male preserve to this day) was Nicholas Lanier, whose lute-playing skills had impressed Charles I. Lanier's role was quite a demanding one: in the 17th century, it was already an established tradition for the monarch to have his or her very own ensemble of musicians (a sort of house band, if you will), and the Master of the King's Musick was required to keep them all in check, to arrange their performances and to inform the monarch's courtiers of their activities. The role quickly grew to include other duties, such as composing birthday or New Year odes, for example. This is how William Boyce came to write his *Symphony No. 2*, a piece regularly heard on Classic FM, with the subtitle *'Ode to the Birthday of Queen Anne'*.

Historically, composers could make quite a decent living from the role of Master of the King's Musick. During the reign of George III, a basic £200-a-year stipend was paid to the incumbent, who could very easily top up his income by composing or performing music for all manner of royal events. Today, however, it is a largely honorary role. The current post-holder, Peter Maxwell Davies, receives a nominal fee, but he is not expected to perform any particular function or compulsorily to provide music for specific occasions, although it is hoped that the composer in question will create music to tie in with significant events in national life. Peter Maxwell Davies has responded by composing various pieces specifically for the Queen, including a work to mark her eightieth birthday in 2006 and a series of Christmas carols in her honour.

The role itself is to music what the poet laureateship is to literature. The royal family's own official website describes the office of Master of the Queen's Music as 'an honour conferred on a musician of great distinction'. So it should be of little surprise that such prestigious composers as Edward Elgar, Arnold Bax and Arthur Bliss held the post during the last century. Elgar used his term of office studiously to track down many of the original instruments that would have been used in the royal band of the Edwardian period; he also set about ensuring that the library of royal music was suitably well stocked.

The invention of the role of Master of the King's Musick was important in the history of classical music for two reasons: firstly, it established a firm link between the royal family and the finest living composers, and secondly, it directly led to the creation of new music, much of which is still performed today. Elgar's delightful *Nursery Suite*, for example, was specifically composed for Princesses Elizabeth and Margaret in 1931, and the present Queen's Coronation in 1953 provided the perfect excuse for two Masters, current and future, to write something entirely new: Arnold Bax, with his *Coronation March for the Queen*, and Arthur Bliss, who composed a special processional in honour of the occasion. For Elizabeth II's Silver Jubilee, Malcolm Williamson (an Australian, and the only Commonwealth citizen to have served as Master of the King's or Queen's Music) wrote his *Mass of Christ the King*, and his *Songs for a Royal Baby* were composed in celebration of the birth of Prince Harry in 1984.

Following the convention established by the fixed-term appointment of Andrew Motion as Poet Laureate in 1999, Peter Maxwell Davies was the first musician to have been appointed for a period of ten years. (Malcolm Williamson had remained in the role from 1975 all the way through to his death in 2003, denying a number of other talented composers their moment in the spotlight.)

As with many royal traditions, there are people who argue that the role of Master of the Queen's Music is a meaningless one. It doesn't demand anything in particular; there isn't a rigorous and heavily scrutinised appointment process, and a number of the former incumbents were hardly household names in their day. But the post offers a unique opportunity for one particular composer to capture the musical spirit of the nation. And in the right hands, it can be used as a great force for good in ensuring that classical music remains an important part of public life – not least in pushing forward the importance of music education in schools. The freedom the Master of the Queen's Music has to write music inspired by and endorsed by royalty is unique – and should not be relinquished lightly. As one of the highest honours that can be bestowed on a British or Commonwealth musician, it's no wonder that so many composers are quietly hoping their turn to hold the post might come soon.

MUSIC AND MOVEMENT: THE FIRST BALLET

Every year at Christmas time, you can be sure that sleigh bells will ring, chestnuts will roast on an open fire and, all around the world, performances of Tchaikovsky's *The Nutcracker* will be staged to the delight of young and old. During other seasons, stages around the globe will play host to scores of different ballets. These will include well-known favourites by composers such as Delibes and Stravinsky, brand new contemporary-dance interpretations and revivals of long-forgotten works. Put simply, the launch of this entire genre around half a millennium ago was one of the most important moments in the history of classical music.

As early as the 1400s, very basic versions of 'dances with music' were being performed in Italy. In those days, the action on the stage was a sort of artistic revue, incorporating everything from poetry and music to visual art and dancing. These were merry affairs, sometimes also including a full meal, with the courses taken between the dances.

To focus in on an exact moment when many historians agree that ballet proper made its first grand entrance, we need to transport ourselves to Paris in 1581. Here, *Le Ballet Comique de la Reine* ('The Comic Ballet of the Queen') was given its inaugural performance. It had been commissioned by Catherine de' Medici (at that time the Queen of France) as part of the celebrations for a royal wedding; the man who staged it went by the wonderfully florid name of Balthasar de Beaujoyeulx. At the time, he could have had no idea that this art form, which he was largely inventing, would go on to become one of the best-loved genres of entertainment the world over. He also evidently knew how to put on one heck of a good party. In the company of around ten thousand guests, he staged a five-hour ballet that didn't even get started until ten o'clock in the evening.

Some historians argue that ballet was already in existence in Renaissance Italy prior to 1581. After all, high-society weddings of the time regularly featured dancers, accompanied by resident court musicians. None of these matched the scale of the ballet staged by the French queen. Having said that, the amount of choreography, as we would think of it today, for the royal event was limited. Nearly all of the modern-day regalia we associate with ballet, from tutus to pointe shoes, were still many years away from becoming a reality. In fact, not a lot of thought had yet gone into the science of ballet; for example, the number of layers worn by the female dancers would have made standing still – let alone dancing – uncomfortable and cumbersome.

At the time of the premiere of *Le Ballet Comique de la Reine*, ballet was practised by enthusiastic amateurs and enjoyed primarily by the royal family or the local aristocracy. Much of the development of a more modern style of ballet took place in France. It took 80 years for any kind of professional organisation for dancers to be established. We have King Louis XIV to thank for the creation of the Académie Royale de Danse in 1681 (later to become the Paris Opéra Ballet). In effect, this was the world's first official ballet company. It initially comprised only men, with female roles being taken by masked male dancers. But by the late 17th century, the Académie included ballerinas among its ranks. Interestingly, although many presume that the exclusion of women was an issue of sexism or tradition, it was, in fact, initially one of physical strength alone. With the requirement to wear huge and elaborate headdresses, heavy corsets and long, thick skirts, there was genuine concern as to whether the lighter female dancers with their small frames would be able to move at all.

The invention of ballet marked a crucial point in the history of music in general, in that it made clear the link between dance and the music of the day. Although there had been musical dance forms in existence for a number of years, the world's first ballet laid the foundations for the formal pairing of music and movement for centuries to come. Over the course of the next 250 years, the medium of ballet would be used as a vehicle of musical expression for some of the most famous composers in history.

When it comes to what we know as ballet in the 21st century, the most rapid developments happened in the 1700s. For a start, the weighty clothing that adorned the dancers began gradually to be removed. Initially, women were covered pretty much from head to toe to preserve their modesty – but a rather bold French dancer called Marie Camargo sounded the death-knell for that approach when, in the 1730s, she wore shortened skirts and heelless slippers to display her dazzling technique. It was only a matter of time before others would follow suit.

Then, as the Romantic era dawned, ballet really came into its own as an art form to be cherished. It was also a means for bringing into existence some of the world's most popular classical music, which was composed specifically for dance. From Tchaikovsky's *The Sleeping Beauty* to Delibes's *Coppélia*, composers, choreographers and librettists collaborated to create lavish, fantastical, fairy-tale ballets, with music that was richly romantic and vividly descriptive. And the development didn't stop there. In the 20th century, Stravinsky caused scandal in Paris and beyond with his *The Rite of Spring* (see Moment No. 27), while Prokofiev's *Romeo and Juliet* was hailed as a masterpiece. Quite some journey for a genre that began all those years ago in the courts of Italy and France. As it is with so many of the aspects of classical music that we discuss in this book, it's a journey that is by no means finished.

BAROQUE 'N' ROLL:
A NEW MUSICAL ERA

As you read through this book, you'll find that certain classical music moments are very easy to pinpoint. The premiere of Beethoven's '*Eroica*', for example, can be dated precisely, as can the invention of the CD or the world's first film score. Other moments we have chosen to include were more gradual and you could even argue that they don't have a home here, due to their being rather more evolutionary than revolutionary. But these developments in classical music were so groundbreaking, so history-changing and so important, that we felt it would be daft to ignore them. No more so is this the case than with the start of the Baroque period.

Classical music can be broken down into a series of different eras and, broadly speaking, when we talk of all things Baroque we're referring to any point from the early 1600s through to about 1750. During this time, it's no exaggeration to say that composers such as J. S. Bach, Handel and

Vivaldi laid the foundations for everything that was to follow in the world of classical music. Opera became really exciting; the modern-day orchestra was born, and the words 'overture' and 'prelude' became part of the musical language. It was also during the Baroque period that concertos were invented, giving a soloist a real chance to show off. In keeping with much of the visual art that was created in the 17th and 18th centuries, the music of the Baroque era is always beautifully crafted, wonderfully melodic and very precise.

During the Renaissance period that preceded all things Baroque, the idea of 'polyphony' (see Moment No. 4) was still a foreign one. Now, however, Baroque composers pushed the musical world forward by writing not just one melody line but a spectacular array of other harmonies to accompany their tune. In doing so, composers made their music more appealing, more accessible and more emotionally charged. Imagine Handel's *'Zadok the Priest'* or Bach's *St Matthew Passion* without any harmonies, and it becomes clear that Baroque music took the building blocks of the Renaissance and added something far more exciting and involving.

The word 'Baroque' comes from the Portuguese word *barroco*, which literally translates as 'strange-shaped pearl'. The term wasn't used at the time but instead entered common usage in the 1800s. It was coined by the critics of the time, who thought the music of this period to be unnecessarily ornate. Originally used in a derogatory way, 'Baroque' has since gone on to be shorthand for some of the most beautiful, most groundbreaking music in the history of the Western world. After all, this was a culturally and artistically rich era – and not just in relation to music. During the Baroque period, Shakespeare was creating the world's most famous literature, Rembrandt was painting visual art that would endure for centuries, and big questions about the meaning of life were being asked by philosophers such as Descartes. Add into this mix the famous names of Baroque music, and you have an exciting, creative melting pot of ideas that would lay the artistic foundations for many years to come.

During the Renaissance, choral works had absolutely dominated the musical world. Come the Baroque period, though, great strides were made outside the choral sphere, and instrumental music became hugely popular. Part of this was due to the fact that classical music was no longer the preserve of the Church. Sacred music was still hugely important, but composers now felt enabled to write secular concertos, operas and early symphonies. This music was then performed in everyday spaces. For the first time, it was common to hear classical music in homes, at parties or in public places, rather than this music remaining the preserve of a musical or religious elite. The development of serious classical music as a medium of entertainment, rather than a part of the liturgy, also meant it became a valuable source of income for musicians. Right across Europe, they were paid to perform at social functions, with the likes of German composer Georg Philipp Telemann making a small fortune from this line of work.

Musical instruments also changed during the Baroque years. In Renaissance times, stringed instruments were rather primitive: viols were modest creations, impressive for their day, but capable of relatively little musical variety. By the time the Classical period began in the mid-18th century, however, the violin, viola and cello were all in regular use. The Baroque period also saw the invention of the harpsichord and thousands of pieces were written for this keyboard instrument, which was essentially the precursor to the piano. Brass, woodwind and percussion instruments all became more complex. These advances opened up myriad musical possibilities, giving composers a far greater palette of sound.

Baroque composers travelled across Europe, sharing exciting new ideas along the way. From Handel and Bach to Rameau and Vivaldi, the Baroque period was home to some of the most famous creators of classical music of all time. The developments they made in terms of the sound of the orchestra, the spreading of this music to the masses, and the invention of entirely new instruments and musical forms provided a crucial springboard to launch the Classical era, during which time the world would see geniuses such as Mozart and Beethoven take these new ideas and run with them – to thrilling effect. Without the Baroque composers putting in the spade work, the Classical and Romantic eras of music would never have turned out the way they did.

A CAPITAL HIT:
HANDEL IN LONDON

At every Coronation since 1727, George Frideric Handel's *'Zadok the Priest'* has been sung. The composer's oratorio *Messiah*, meanwhile, is one of the most performed pieces of music in the world. George I commissioned Handel's *Water Music Suites*, and George II stumped up the cash for the *Music for the Royal Fireworks*. In other words, to say that this German-born composer had a significant effect on the musical life of England would be the definition of an understatement. We therefore feel justified in saying that Handel's move to London in 1712 was one of the most significant moments in the history of classical music in the UK.

Handel was born in the German city of Halle in February 1685 – but history does not remember him as a German composer. The reason? A number of years after his move to London, Handel applied for British citizenship, which he was successfully granted on 20 February 1727. In many ways, Handel relished playing the role of the archetypal British composer. Beloved of the Establishment, he regularly wrote music for the great and the good, having first been granted a royal pension of £200 (quite a sum in those days) by Queen Anne in December 1713. He willingly composed music in English – his oratorio *Esther*, for example – and was a major player on the London concert scene.

Handel was only in his mid-twenties when he arrived in London, and it was an incredibly exciting place for the young composer to live and work. The city was home to around a million people. As is the case today, it was a vibrant, cosmopolitan place, teeming with ideas, art and culture. Handel's first opera for the London season, *Rinaldo*, was a resounding success, and it is fitting that the city's most iconic shopping destination, Harrods, now uses the famous aria from *Rinaldo*, *'Lascia ch'io pianga'*, as the theme tune to its television and radio advertising campaign. After the first run of this new opera, Handel had to travel to Hanover, much to the disappointment of his London fans. He had not yet moved to London for good; when he returned, the music-loving public was incredibly keen for him to make England his long-term home. One William Coxe, who knew Handel relatively well by virtue of being the stepson of the composer's amanuensis, commented at the time, 'His return to London was hailed by the musical world as a national acquisition, and every measure was adopted to make his abode pleasant and permanent.'

The house in which Handel eventually lived, from 1723 until his death in 1759, was on Brook Street in Mayfair. This central, desirable location was the perfect place for Handel to compose his many masterpieces, and it enabled him to embed himself very deeply into England's musical life. His move to London was highly significant because without it many of the composer's most feted pieces of music would never have been written. Take, for example, 'Zadok the Priest': this most English of works was commissioned for the Coronation of King George II. Had Handel remained a German citizen, it's unthinkable that the monarchy would have approached him to write the piece.

Handel very much filled a void in England's musical life. The last truly great English composer, Henry Purcell, had died in 1695, and the country lacked another innovative, exciting musical voice. This German genius delighted British audiences, whether through his position as composer to the Chapel Royal, awarded in 1723, or his role conducting his own operas. He was also a commercially savvy man, making an awful lot of money during his lifetime, not least because he had a great instinct for what London audiences wanted to hear. When, for example, the appetite for opera appeared to be on the wane in the 1740s, Handel turned his attention to oratorios instead. And, as a consequence, he composed one of the most famous pieces in the history of all classical music: *Messiah*.

This wonderful oratorio was actually first performed in Dublin in 1742 – but Handel didn't wait long before introducing it to London audiences the following year. Astonishingly, it took him only 21 days to compose. Within Handel's own lifetime, *Messiah* was given a further 35 performances and, today, it is sung thousands of times around the world every single year. Handel would always insist on an annual charitable performance of the work, to raise money for the Foundling Hospital – a children's home in Bloomsbury. As well as his musical contribution to London life, Handel made an enormously generous financial contribution to the city, too. His annual concerts raised around £7,000 which, in the 18th century, was the equivalent of half a million pounds. He also paid for an organ to be installed in the Foundling Hospital chapel, thus ensuring it would be possible for his music to be performed there for many years to come. In his will, Handel left £1,000 to the Fund for the Support of Decay'd Musicians, a charity that assisted musicians or their close relatives in old age.

Without his move to London, Handel would have almost certainly found a happy home in another European city. As a twenty-something composer, he was already bright, talented and set for a very exciting future. He could have settled anywhere, but chose London. And that decision back in 1712 ensured that England's musical life took a distinct turn for the better.

RELIGIOUS CHANGE:
MARTIN LUTHER AND
THE PROTESTANT REFORMATION

Many of the moments we've picked in this book are understandably very musical in nature. But this particular event doesn't just represent a seismic shift in classical music; it's one of the most significant moments in the history of the Western world. The Protestant Reformation had far-ranging ramifications culturally, politically and religiously. A by-product of this was that European music would never be the same again.

Martin Luther, the man who spearheaded the Reformation, was a fine musician in his own right. He played both the flute and the lute; he was an exceptionally good tenor and he also found the time to compose. Luther's own view of music was a very spiritual one. He believed that 'the gift of language combined with the gift of song was given to man only that he should praise God with both words and music, mainly by proclaiming the Word of God through music and by providing sweet melodies with words'. Luther's love of music had been fostered from a young age. He spent his early years in the German city of Thuringia, a place known at the time for being a centre of music-making. By the time he turned fifteen, Luther was regularly singing in a local choir and performing at church services, weddings and funerals. So in 1505, when he became a monk, it seemed only natural for Luther to choose the Augustine brotherhood, an order that was well known for its musicianship.

One of the core Protestant beliefs at the forefront of the Reformation was the concept of 'The Priesthood of All Believers'. Essentially, this was the notion that every Christian could come before God and that all were equal in His sight, no matter what their formal religious training or holy order. Music played an integral part in this. Luther believed that the Church should return to its roots and include the entire congregation in its sung worship. He took well-known sacred German Lieder, or songs, and used them as a form of collective, all-embracing praise. Hymns and chorales became a central part of church services, and they used relatively simple classical melodies.

It would be true to say that, by the time of the Reformation, much of the music to have come from the Catholic Church was, while undeniably beautiful, not particularly accessible for the average German on the street. The complex, interwoven music of Catholicism certainly sounded heavenly, but it wasn't something that encouraged participation. In his new churches, Luther took an entirely different approach. Ordinary churchgoers began to experience sung worship for the first time – something that inevitably led to a greater musical literacy among congregations.

Luther's high personal regard for music was absolutely crucial in bringing these changes about. He regularly spoke of this publicly, once stating:

> Music is a fair and lovely gift of God which has often wakened and moved me to the joy of preaching . . . I have no use for cranks who despise music, because it is a gift of God. Music drives away the devil . . . My heart bubbles up and overflows in response to music, which has so often refreshed me and delivered me from dire plagues.

The effect of the Reformation wasn't felt only within the churches, though. Instead, it affected the whole of society: young people were educated in the rudiments of sacred music from an early age, meaning it became part and parcel of their childhood. Luther's aim was to make music a central element of every Protestant's life, primarily as an act of worship. Unsurprisingly, this was exactly what happened in a great many cases, but even those who didn't choose to follow the faith as adults still had the benefit of a wonderful musical grounding.

Luther also fought hard for the state funding of music education. He was passionate about enabling the German people to experience sacred music in their own language. Up until that point, Latin had been the dominant language in the Catholic Church, but from the Reformation onwards, it became possible for people to take part in the tradition of the Mass in German. Luther himself presided over the first German Mass on 29 October 1525 – and every aspect of it, from the traditional melodies to the actual words, was German.

It's crucial to remember that the Reformation occurred well before the time of most famous classical composers. Consequently, Luther was laying the foundations for the likes of Handel and J. S. Bach, both of whom composed outstanding sacred works that went on to attract widespread public appeal. Luther did not personally invent wholly new musical forms – far from it. Instead, he took the existing structures, such as the Mass, and found a way of making them accessible and involving for the average German citizen.

The democratisation of music that came about as part of the Reformation spread well beyond Germany. By 1640, more than a million copies of the Protestant book of sung psalms had been printed in England and Scotland. At that time, a great many people were illiterate, and this new approach of encouraging everyone to sing together was a vital way of introducing them to the written version of their mother tongue. These psalms also found life as a kind of protest song, as the battle between Protestantism and Catholicism continued to rage. At the downfall of the Catholic Mary Queen of Scots in 1567, the Scottish Protestants sang from the psalms, *'Judge and revenge my cause, O Lord, from them that evil be'*. Just one of the direct consequences of the Reformation that stretched far beyond Luther's initial movement for change in Germany.

WORDS AND MUSIC: THE FIRST OPERA

From Puccini's 'Nessun Dorma' from *Turandot*, made famous to millions through its use in the Italia '90 World Cup (see Moment No. 42), to Verdi's *Grand March* from *Aida* and Mascagni's beautiful *Intermezzo* from *Cavalleria rusticana*, some of the finest and most popular tunes in all classical music derive from the world of opera. Without this particular art form, we would be deprived of a great deal of wonderful music we've come to know and love, so it's fair to say that the invention of opera was a pretty momentous occurrence.

At the time it happened, in 1597, the composer Jacopo Peri would have had no idea just how much his latest work was going to change the history of classical music. He was 36 years old and had come from a privileged background; Peri was from noble stock and had a fine musical training, going on to work for a series of members of the ruling classes including the Duke of Tuscany. He was also part of the intelligentsia of Florence; his close circle of friends included a number of artists and writers, all of whom shared his interest in Greek tragedy.

Consequently, it's no surprise that he chose to collaborate with the poet Ottavio Rinuccini to compose a drama (or an opera, as it would go on to be described) entitled *Dafne*. Its first performance was not in a lavish opera house – unsurprising, really, given that such venues didn't exist yet – but in the opulent, private surroundings of Florence's Palazzo Corsi. Before long, news of this new art form had spread, and the duo of Peri and Rinuccini were commissioned to create another opera, this time in celebration of the marriage in France of Henri IV and his fiancée Marie de' Medici. Although *Dafne* was the world's very first opera, it was this follow-up, *L'Euridice*, that really became something of a starting point for other composers, who were soon to set about writing operas of their own.

Given Peri's admirable success in creating an entirely new genre, expectations for what he would do next were inevitably high; it might have been expected that opera after opera would flow from his pen. Sadly, though, Peri pretty much disappeared without trace. After becoming the music master to the Duke of Ferrara in 1601, he went on to publish some further musical writings, but following that, nothing more is known of him. Even more disappointingly, all records of *Dafne* are now completely lost, so we're sadly unable to discover what the world's first opera would have sounded like in any great detail.

What we do know, however, is that this new style of music was noticeable for how obviously it broke away from some of the traditions of its day. At that time, composers such as Palestrina were all the rage. They wrote polyphonic music – in other words, music with lots of different, interweaving lines and melodies – and this was what the Italian public was used to hearing (see Moment No. 4). In *Dafne*, however, because he needed to set the words of individual characters to music, Peri would have taken a much more singular or 'monodic' approach. So, in composing *Dafne*, he wasn't just creating the world's first opera; he was also playing his part in ushering in a new way of writing music altogether.

Many of the operatic 'hits' we know today are arias – individual songs performed by the main characters (more often than not, the soprano or the tenor). In Peri's day, though, the aria had yet to develop. In fact, nearly all of *L'Euridice* was made up of recitative: the quickly delivered, almost spoken sections of the opera that exist to tell large parts of the story in a short space of time. As a result, although *L'Euridice* was appreciated for its novelty factor, it wasn't actually an especially memorable opera.

Thankfully, however, one particularly gifted composer had got wind of what Peri was up to, and he decided to get in on the opera act himself, to rather fantastic effect. His name? Claudio Monteverdi. And Monteverdi's opera *Orfeo*, composed in 1607, was the first truly to use what we might describe today as 'arias'. Instead of just employing the music as a mechanism to tell a story, Monteverdi understood the importance of including some beautiful melodies along the way, and by using a few Italian tunes that were already well established in popular culture, he ensured that *Orfeo* would be a hit.

It was not until the Classical period, though, that opera really became a staple of the musical world. Admittedly, various composers from Gluck to Handel did write operas – and often relatively successful ones, at that – but opera absolutely came into its own from Mozart's time onwards. Wolfgang Amadeus himself contributed a huge amount to the genre: *The Marriage of Figaro*, *The Magic Flute* and *Così fan tutte* are just three of his operatic success stories, and all are still very regularly performed around the world today. Then, once the Romantic period dawned in the 19th century, opera provided the perfect vehicle for all that raw emotion and heart-on-your-sleeve expression that was just waiting to burst out. From Puccini and Verdi to Bizet and Wagner, many of the era's most famous composers expressed their very best music through the medium of opera.

Were the audience at that very first performance of *Dafne* in Florence to attend an opera today, the chances are they wouldn't even begin to recognise the similarities between Peri's creation and what they would see on the stage in front of them now. Opera has come a very long way from its earliest awakenings in 16th-century Italy.

THE WORLD'S GREATEST OPERA HOUSE: LA SCALA, MILAN

As a country, Italy is the home of opera – and, as a venue, La Scala in Milan is arguably the most important building in the history of this great art form. Since 1778, it has housed hundreds of premieres, welcomed a stellar line-up of famous composers and performers, and continues to be the place where opera lovers around the world flock to hear their favourite music performed at the highest possible quality. So, we feel confident in saying that the building of La Scala in the late 18th century represents one of the most important moments in the history of classical music.

Anyone doubting the significance of La Scala needs only to look at the list of operatic premieres that have taken place there over the last couple of hundred years. The composer Giuseppe Verdi owes much of his international fame to La Scala, where his operas *Nabucco*, *Otello* and *Falstaff* were all premiered. Verdi by no means always had an easy ride at La Scala. The conservative audience there couldn't be relied on to welcome his music and, for quite some time, he chose to premiere his operas elsewhere. Nevertheless, La Scala had a pull on Verdi that the composer simply couldn't ignore. It wasn't just Verdi, though. La Scala was the venue for the premieres of countless famous operas, including Bellini's *Norma*, Puccini's *Turandot* and Rossini's *Italian Girl in Algiers*.

La Scala opened in the summer of 1778 with a performance of the now relatively unknown Salieri opera *Europa riconosciuta*. Up until this point, Italy hadn't been known for producing the kind of music that involved large symphony orchestras or big-name conductors. That was all set to change, though, and La Scala became the place to witness some of the brightest talent in action.

Wind forward to the 20th century and La Scala was home to many of the world's most famous conductors, including the great Arturo Toscanini, who held the position of Artistic Director. During his tenure, he championed the operas of Wagner in Italy and developed the orchestra in its own right. Toscanini's long association with La Scala had begun when, at the age of nineteen, he played the cello in the orchestra at the premiere performance of Verdi's *Otello*. As late as 1948, he conducted the gala reopening of La Scala after extensive refurbishment works; visitors can still see a bust of the great conductor in the foyer. And during the last century, regular appearances by the likes of Leonard Bernstein, Carlos Kleiber and Carlo Maria Giulini helped to cement La Scala's position as the world's most exciting and dynamic opera house.

La Scala, Milan – or, to give it its Italian title, Teatro alla Scala – came into existence as a result of some fairly unfortunate circumstances. In 1776, the city's Teatro Ducale opera house had burned down, so the architect Giuseppe Piermarini was commissioned to create La Scala as a replacement. Today, thousands of visitors flock to the venue each year, not just to marvel at the music but also to appreciate the stunning architecture. The on-site Museum of La Scala offers an opportunity to view documents, busts and portraits featuring everyone from Puccini to Verdi, alongside exhibitions that pay homage to contemporary stars of the operatic world.

The building of La Scala in 1778 was a landmark moment in the history of opera – but it's not just a historical curiosity. The importance of the venue today should not be underestimated. In 2010, led by the great Daniel Barenboim, hundreds of protesters took to the streets of Milan to campaign against the Italian government's proposed cuts in arts funding, which were set to impact La Scala directly. In 2006, Barenboim had been made the Principal Guest Conductor of La Scala and, never afraid of making a political statement, the Argentine-Israeli musician used the opportunity to publicly declare his support for La Scala and for the arts in general in Italy. Speaking at a performance of Wagner's *Die Walküre*, in the presence of the then Italian president, Giorgio Napolitano, Barenboim declared, 'For that title, and also in the names of the colleagues who play, sing, dance and work, not only here but in all theatres, I am here to tell you we are deeply worried for the future of culture in the country and in Europe.' Barenboim went on to read Article 9 of the

Italian Constitution, which refers to governments safeguarding Italy's 'historical and artistic heritage' – a clear reference to the importance of La Scala in terms of the country's contribution to classical music in the world at large.

Fans of the Metropolitan Opera in New York or the Royal Opera House in London's Covent Garden might well question why La Scala should be marked out above those illustrious venues. Wonderful as they both are, the number of operatic premieres La Scala has hosted serves to highlight how, without it, the very existence of some of the world's greatest operas could well have been in doubt. Even to this day, the operatic repertoire performed at La Scala is deliberately broad. The popular favourites do feature, but they are nearly always outnumbered by lesser-known works. La Scala can sell out pretty much any opera or ballet it stages; consequently, it offers a huge amount of artistic freedom to its musicians. Conductors aren't just expected to turn up for rehearsals: they are given total control of casting, too – something that is by no means the norm at every other major opera house in the world.

It's not just composers, but major operatic performers who have made their mark on the stage at La Scala – none more so than the great soprano Maria Callas. Local opera aficionados in Milan took quite some time to embrace Callas; but when, in 1950, she performed in Verdi's *The Sicilian Vespers* for the opening night of the season, the audience erupted with enthusiasm and she was taken to their hearts. Since then, the biggest operatic names, from Luciano Pavarotti to Angela Gheorghiu, have found La Scala to be their operatic home.

If you ever find yourself in Milan, do pay La Scala a visit. But if you want to attend an opera, you'll need to be pretty organised. Tickets sell out months in advance. That's not surprising, though; this is the world's greatest opera house, after all.

CLASSIC DISCOVERY:
ANOTHER ERA OF CHANGE

In Moment No. 11, we saw how the foundations of modern-day classical music were laid during the Baroque era. From the mid-18th century onwards, the musical world became even more revolutionary, with the composers of the Classical period building on those Baroque ideas, as well as coming up with plenty of entirely new ones all of their own. Along the way, they created some truly wonderful music.

As we said in our chapter about the Baroque period, musical eras can't always be neatly segmented into absolutely exact spans, with classical music constantly evolving over time. So, once again, we're viewing this moment as being one that lasted a while.

The Classical period took over in the mid-1700s, as the Baroque era began to wind down. The dawning of the new musical era saw the emergence of some key defining characteristics. Where the music of the Baroque period was ordered, efficient and complex, the new sound of the Classical period tended to focus on simplifying things a little bit – but also making them bigger. This might sound like a contradiction in terms, but we promise you that it's not as illogical as it might at first appear.

On a purely stylistic level, there was simply more to hum along to in the Classical period. Melodies and plain good tunes took over from complex polyphony, and composers such as Haydn and Mozart flourished because they were so good at writing these melodic hits. It's highly likely that you already know a great many of Mozart's tunes, even if you're not aware that they were written by him. If in doubt, have a quick listen to the opening of *Eine kleine Nachtmusik*, the Overture to *The Marriage of Figaro* or the first move-ment of the *Symphony No. 40* and, the chances are, you'll be convinced.

In Baroque times, the development of harmony had been hugely exciting; during the Classical era, attention turned once again to the supremacy of the melody. It became the most important thing to get right – and it was a task that the composers of the day absolutely relished.

As in Baroque times, developments came thick and fast, not just in the way classical music was constructed, but also to the instruments that were making the music, too. They constantly changed as various bright sparks came up with handy innovations – not least the piano (see Moment No. 1), which replaced the Baroque period's harpsichord as the must-have instrument of the day. Another major change during this time related to the orchestra: during the late 18th and early 19th centuries, it underwent significant expansion. As new instruments were invented and old ones improved, they were absorbed into the Classical orchestra. For the first time, there was an entire woodwind section of flutes, clarinets, oboes and bassoons, rather than a lone Baroque flute playing alongside a string ensemble and a horn or two. And with a large number of symphonies now being composed, the orchestra started to resemble the kind of musical groupings we see in concert halls today.

During the Classical period, the range of music that was being composed expanded massively. There were more symphonies, concertos, solo instrumental pieces and operas than ever before. It wasn't only about Mozart and Haydn, either: in addition to other big-name composers such as Rossini and Paganini, Beethoven began writing music during the Classical period. He would go on to stretch and, ultimately, break the Classical mould, with his often deeply emotional or political symphonies growing to relatively mammoth proportions.

The Classical era gave birth to works for smaller forces, too. Take, for example, the many piano sonatas composed by Mozart and the emergence of the string quartet, with Haydn one of the major innovators in this area. Much of this music was written with the express purpose of being performed in ordinary places, as the middle classes across Europe embraced the idea of classical music being part of their lifestyle. In essence, whether in large-scale symphonies and operas or intimate chamber pieces, the Classical period is the sound of delicate order gradually being taken over by emotion and indulgence.

As time went on, classical music's sound became more and more full-blooded and emotionally expressive – leading perfectly into the aptly named Romantic period that followed. By the time the likes of Beethoven and Schubert were writing their later pieces in the early 19th century, the neat structures of the Classical period were bursting at the seams. Just as the early Classical composers sought to push the boundaries of the Baroque, so these late Classical masters were struggling to convey all their musical ideas within the very rigid formats and structures of their period. Unsurprisingly, the years that followed became all about rewriting the rule book of the Classical era, bringing a more expansive and emotional sound to the music, and stretching the orchestra in a variety of new ways. Unlike the two eras that preceded it, the Romantic period was heralded at one very specific point, which we cover in Moment No. 20. But, without their Classical predecessors, these Romantic composers would have had much less to build on – and no structures from which to break free. Even though the music of the Classical era deserves to be lauded for its own sake, for this reason, the entire period is a moment worth marking, and its relevance still resounds across the musical world today.

THE INSTRUMENT-
MAKER EXTRAORDINAIRE:
ANTONIO STRADIVARI

We all know the phrase 'a workman is only as good as his tools' – and in the world of classical music, that analogy rings true just as much as it does in every other area of life. Nigel Kennedy might well be one of the greatest ever violinists, but put a sub-standard instrument in his hands and even he will struggle to create that near-perfect, pure sound for which he's known and loved. And when it comes to stringed instruments, the birth of one particular man in 1644 paved the way for a seismic moment in musical history, after which violins would never sound the same again.

Antonio Stradivari was born in the town of Cremona in Italy, where he lived and worked for his entire life. His skill as an instrument-maker was honed under the tutelage of a local craftsman by the name of Nicolò Amati. Stradivari lived well into his nineties – a remarkably long life for someone born in the 17th century – and, over the course of his 70-year career, his instruments became the most desirable, most prized possessions in classical music. After having trained as a luthier, Stradivari set about creating the most amazing stringed instruments. His violins, in particular, were renowned for their beautiful tone, and musicians would travel for thousands of miles from across Europe in order to be the proud owner of one of them. Stradivari's shop in Cremona became the go-to place for any musician who could afford the very best instrument. In addition to his violins, Stradivari made harps, viols, mandolins and cellos. Over the course of his career, he personally crafted well over a thousand instruments. Today, around six hundred of them are still in use, and these highly prized 'Strads', as they're known, change hands for millions of pounds.

Within his lifetime, Stradivari was a sensation: his competitors would desperately try to discover his secret, as they attempted in vain to emulate the master's success. Even today, it would be fair to say that no one is quite sure exactly what makes a Strad so special, or how this master craftsman managed to create such a wonderful sound. Stradivari would regularly try out new ideas, altering the specific thickness of the wood or experimenting with the precise varnish he used to finish off the instrument in question. These were beautiful creations – but very sturdy ones, too, and the fact that hundreds of them survive to this day is testament to their creator's expert approach.

The golden period as far as Stradivari was concerned was at the start of the 1700s. By this time, he had spent a number of decades honing and perfecting his art, and his reputation as the master instrument-maker of his generation had already been cemented. Demand for Stradivari's instruments was huge, but he still took the same amount of time, care and effort to create every single one of them. He would employ others in his workshop, of course – not least his sons, Omobono and Francesco – but they were monitored very closely to ensure that the exacting Stradivari sound was still heard from every single instrument that left the building. Each one of them was marked with the Latin inscription 'Antonius Stradivarius Cremonensis Faciebat Anno [x]', translating as 'Antonio Stradivari, Cremona, made in the year [x]'.

Today, the announcement that a Strad has become available on the market results in a huge amount of excitement. At public auctions, these instruments command huge sums. One of the most prized Stradivarius violins in the world, nicknamed the 'Lady Blunt', sold for just under £10 million in the summer of 2011. Another, known as 'The Messiah', has been on display in the Ashmolean Museum in Oxford since 1939 and was played by some of the outstanding violinists of the 19th and early 20th centuries, including Pablo de Sarasate and Yehudi Menuhin. In the 21st century, meanwhile, many of our finest string players are proud owners of one of Stradivari's instruments. The great violinist Itzhak Perlman owns a Strad that dates from 1714 (slap bang in the middle of Stradivari's most creative and productive period). And world-class performers on other stringed instruments are equally keen to be in possession of one: Yo-Yo Ma owns the 'Davidov' Strad cello, and his fellow cellist Mstislav Rostropovich would nearly always perform on one of Stradivari's creations.

In the three centuries since Antonio Stradivari began crafting his instruments, classical music has undergone a huge range of developments. In the case of the violin, the instruments performed on today often bear very little resemblance to those that left Stradivari's workshop in Cremona. Over time, as playing standards have changed and the range of the violin (in other words, the number of notes that can be played on it) has been extended, Stradivari's instruments have been subjected to the musical equivalent of a rather large house extension. New fingerboards have been added, additional pegs have been put in place to enable the strings to be adjusted, and in many cases the instruments have been made larger. Some would argue this is a shame, but in nearly all cases, the evolution in the sound and shape of a Strad has been handled with the utmost care. Had these instruments been left as historical museum pieces, they would not have continued to be played by musicians across the world – and Antonio Stradivari himself would have surely loathed the idea of his beautiful violins and cellos never actually being used for the purpose for which they were intended.

Antonio Stradivari was not a composer or performer. He is not remembered for his wonderful music, his outstanding interpretations, or his legendary recordings. But hundreds of years after his birth, instrument-makers and scientists alike are still trying to fathom exactly what it is that makes a Strad so special – and that is surely the highest compliment that could be paid to the man from Cremona.

TAKING THE ORCHESTRA
TO ANOTHER LEVEL:
HECTOR BERLIOZ

The Romantic period of classical music was not a time that was especially well known for the invention of new musical instruments. Instead, the 19th century was of particular significance because composers began to use the instruments that had appeared in the previous century to their full potential. Everything from the piano to the violin was being stretched to show the extremes of each instrument's capabilities. As designs and manufacture became more refined, and as virtuosic soloists honed their skills, the relationship between performer and instrument was taken to new heights of artistic excellence.

One thing that really *did* change during the Romantic period, though, was the sheer size of the orchestra and the way in which all these instruments could be blended together to make the most remarkable new sounds. And the one man who could lay claim to taking this approach to greater heights than any other was the French composer Hector Berlioz.

Composing mainly in the mid-1800s, Berlioz was obsessed with the orchestra. His landmark 1855 publication, the *Grand Treaty on Instruments and Modern Orchestration*, contained a set of entirely fresh ideas about how an orchestra could be structured and used in all its musical glory. Many of Berlioz's own pieces were among the most forward-thinking works of their time. For example, his *Roman Carnival Overture* used extremes of sound, volume and texture that took the orchestra to a new level, setting the pace for the composers who were to come. In his treaty, Berlioz comprehensively outlined exactly how the instruments of the orchestra should be grouped; he also used a large number of examples from the works of his predecessors, including Gluck and Beethoven, to show exactly what he meant by this. It was an exhaustive accomplishment, still thought of today as one of the most important reference points in the history of the symphony orchestra.

Berlioz also used the full forces of the Romantic orchestra to tell fantastical stories in an unashamedly heart-on-his-sleeve way. At nearly an hour in length, his orchestral tone poem *Symphonie fantastique* was one of the first pieces of its kind, designed to tell an epic story through music. Covering everything from impassioned love to dark witchcraft, the *Symphonie fantastique* is rather like a musical opium-induced trip, incorporating the sound of a severed head falling into a basket, a funeral gathering of ghouls and monsters, and a witches' dance. In his own programme notes dating from

1845, Berlioz described his extraordinary creation in a way that serves to highlight his extreme, florid approach:

> The author imagines that a young vibrant musician, afflicted by the sickness of spirit which a famous writer has called the wave of passions, sees for the first time a woman who unites all the charms of the ideal person his imagination was dreaming of, and falls desperately in love with her . . . The transitions from this state of dreamy melancholy, interrupted by occasional upsurges of aimless joy, to delirious passion, with its outbursts of fury and jealousy, its returns of tenderness, its tears, its religious consolations – all this forms the subject of the first movement.

Berlioz's unique, groundbreaking approach was driven home in many of his other compositions – not least his perennially popular *Hungarian March*, an 1846 piece that uses the range of the symphony orchestra in a way that, at the time, was incredibly exciting for audiences in the concert hall. Previously, it had been a generally accepted norm that the string section would begin an orchestral piece, before other performers joined in. Here, though, Berlioz kicks in straight away with a fanfare from the brass – an arresting opening that immediately demonstrated to listeners that Berlioz was determined to make a statement and do something different. All of a sudden, the brass, woodwind and percussion seem to be given equal billing to the strings, making the critics of the day sit up and take note of what this hugely confident French composer was doing. In taking such an approach, Berlioz legitimised using the orchestra in revolutionary ways. Soon afterwards, a host of other Romantic-era composers would follow suit. Many of the concepts Berlioz introduced were developed by Wagner, who was a great admirer of Berlioz's music – as was Franz Liszt.

Generally speaking, however, Berlioz was not particularly celebrated in his native France during his own lifetime. It's only in the last 50 years that his status and importance in the history of classical music has been properly credited, not least as a result of a major project to record everything Berlioz ever composed, undertaken by the much missed British conductor Colin Davis.

Berlioz was often dismissed as something of an arrogant eccentric, sometimes by his fellow composers. Mendelssohn wrote in a letter to his family in 1830:

He makes me really sad, because he is actually a cultured, agreeable man and yet he composed so incredibly badly . . . deaf to any outside criticism in his determination to follow only his inner inspiration.

Many of those critics were from an earlier school of thought. Still clinging on to the last vestiges of the Classical period, they saw Berlioz's orchestral magic as being too indulgent or experimental, when he was, in fact, a great musical innovator, almost single-handedly displaying just what could now be done with the might of the orchestra that lay before him. Berlioz was clearly a significant figure in the history of classical music. By shaking up the orchestra, stretching it to its full potential and showing other composers the rich possibilities of its sound, texture and force, he ensured that the symphony orchestra would never be the same again. As the likes of Mahler and Wagner were to go on to demonstrate just a few years later, once Berlioz had smashed his way through the barricades, there really was no turning back.

THE WORLD'S FIRST CLASSICAL MUSIC SUPERSTAR: FRANZ LISZT

I f you imagined that classical music must have always been a very polite affair during the 19th century, prepare to think again. For, in the late 1830s, one particular composer revolutionised the way in which classical music concerts were presented, making himself something of a heart-throb in the process.

Franz Liszt was born in Hungary in 1811. Even before his birth, there were suggestions that this child was going to be very special. A gypsy predicted to Liszt's mother, Anna Maria, that the baby she was carrying would turn out to be an exceptional talent. Within a few years of his birth, it was clear that the young Franz was indeed on the path to greatness. Liszt initially studied the piano under the direction of his father, Adam, a talented musician in his own right, who could count Beethoven, Hummel and Haydn among his friends. Recognising his son's abilities, Liszt Senior later arranged for his boy to study the piano in Vienna with the composers Antonio Salieri and Carl Czerny.

Fast-forward to 1839, and Liszt was in his late twenties. By this point, he had become determined to change the art of concert performance completely, and he set off on a tour across Europe buoyed up by super-charged levels of confidence, bravura and talent that would enable him to do exactly that. At this point, no serious musician believed for a moment that the performer himself was a star: by contrast, the accepted wisdom of the time stated that it was the music that should take centre stage. The performer was merely a vehicle to express whatever the composer desired; his or her job was to deflect any attention from the soloist to the music in question. Liszt, however, had other ideas. He was blessed with good looks and, bluntly, he saw no reason why he could not exploit them to make the art of performance a more theatrical and, therefore, exciting experience for all concerned.

The first step the young composer and pianist took was to alter the location of the piano on the concert-hall stage. Up until this point, the instrument was positioned facing the orchestra. In other words, it was virtually impossible for any member of the audience to see the soloist in action. Liszt changed all that, though, placing the piano in profile to the audience. All of a sudden, people could see his hands, his gestures, and his facial expressions. Liszt also decided to dispense with the unnecessary baggage of sheet music. Again, this was revolutionary: previously, to play without music was ridiculed, but Liszt realised there was simply no need to walk on stage with sheets of paper if he already knew what he would be playing off by heart.

Liszt's entirely new approach didn't stop there, though: he was also the first pianist to walk on from the side of the stage on his own at the start of the concert, and he invented the very term 'recital'. When we consider the nature of a piano-led concert today, whether it's Stephen Hough dazzling us with a concerto at the Royal Albert Hall or Lang Lang delighting a stadium full of fans in China, a lot of what they do harks back to Franz Liszt.

The results of Liszt's modernisations to the way pianists performed were dramatic. He also had the most remarkable effect on members of his audience, particularly women. There are reports of ladies stuffing Liszt's used cigar butts down their cleavages and fights breaking out over who would take home his discarded handkerchiefs. Such was the adulation for the composer, Liszt even demanded that seats be removed in the concert halls in which he played. After all, the atmosphere there was more like a rock gig, with members of the audience jumping up and down and exclaiming with pleasure – making any form of seating utterly superfluous.

All this led to one concert reviewer dubbing the new-found phenomenon 'Lisztomania'. Writing about Liszt's 1844 season in Berlin, Heinrich Heine commented, 'I explained this Lisztomania . . . how convulsively his mere appearance affected them! How boisterous was the applause which rang to meet him! What acclaim it was! A veritable insanity, one unheard of in the annals of furore.' At that time, Lisztomania was genuinely considered to be a medical condition and there was considerable concern that the women swooning over the composer were affected by something more than momentary lust. The appearance of Liszt in any local concert hall was therefore considered something of a health hazard.

By this point, Franz Liszt's place in history was well and truly secured. He had become the world's first musical superstar, beginning a trend that would continue to this day in the classical world but, crucially, would also branch out into every other musical genre. From now on, it was no longer inherently wrong to pay close attention to the soloist, or to express delight in his or her performance. On the contrary, the concept of the musician as star only increased during the Romantic period, with soloists now permitted to claim their moment in the spotlight.

By changing the way in which the piano was placed on the stage, Liszt took a definite step towards making classical concerts all the more accessible. Even today, first-time concertgoers are welcomed into the world of classical music far more effectively when they can watch as well as hear the soloist. So, next time you're sitting waiting for a recital to begin, or you see a pianist walk on stage, or you catch Elton John playing the piano on the television with his instrument placed in profile to the orchestra, spare a thought for Franz Liszt. Without him, it might never have happened.

ROMANTICISM ARRIVES: BEETHOVEN'S *EROICA*

For some people, Beethoven's *Symphony No. 3* (*'Eroica'*) represents the pinnacle of the Classical period. We prefer to see the premiere of this mighty symphony as significant not so much because it marked the end of one classical musical era but because it heralded the triumphant beginning of a new one altogether.

'I am not satisfied with my works up to the present time,' wrote Beethoven to a friend in 1802. 'From today, I mean to take a new road.' This he most certainly did, by creating a symphony so radical that it continues to be one of the most important works in the entire classical music repertoire. From the very first movement, with its two arresting opening chords (with which Beethoven apparently wanted to shock audiences), through to the multiple and innovative settings of the main themes throughout, this was unlike anything that had been composed before.

Beethoven's *Symphony No. 3* was first performed on

7 April 1805 and, in the history of music, it has come to represent the flowering of a whole host of ideas about what a symphony should sound like. Emotion had certainly been expressed within the music of the Classical period, but there had always been a sense that structure, equilibrium and order were the hallmarks of a good piece of music. Now, in the 'Eroica', Beethoven displayed emotion, tension and passion in a far more intense way than audiences had been used to hearing. It was clear that times were changing – and that Beethoven was at the forefront of ushering in something new.

It's worth bearing in mind that although this symphony is among the most performed of all classical works in the concert hall today, at the time it left a great many listeners completely bemused. Don't forget: contemporary audiences were used to symphonies lasting, on average, around 25 minutes. With the 'Eroica' coming in at something like double that, many people simply didn't understand what Beethoven was trying to do, dismissing him as trying and failing to strive for musical originality. One reviewer, while admitting that he noticed Beethoven's 'very daring ideas . . . very powerfully carried out', dismissed the 'Eroica' on account of its 'inordinate length and extreme difficulty of execution'.

Another critic of the time argued that 'the endless duration of this longest and perhaps most difficult of all symphonies is tiring even for the expert; for the mere amateur it is unbearable'. It was also a deeply political piece: it reflected Beethoven's musical response to what was happening in the world around him. Nowadays, it's all too easy for us to place the great composers of the past on a pedestal, revering them as godlike figures who were above the day-to-day business of the world. As Beethoven proved here, though, that couldn't be further from the truth.

The *'Eroica'* was dedicated originally to Napoleon, whose new constitution founded on 'the true principles of representative government, on the sacred rights of property, equality, and liberty' had impressed the composer. But when Beethoven discovered that Napoleon had declared himself Emperor, he made his displeasure known. The result of all this was that Beethoven scrapped the idea of associating the *'Eroica'* with Napoleon, deciding instead to name the piece the *'Sinfonia Eroica'* or 'Heroic Symphony' and dedicating it to 'the memory of a great man'.

Once the *'Eroica'* had received its premiere, there really was no going back. Beethoven was already firmly established as one of Europe's most exciting and influential composers, and a work of such groundbreaking nature was impossible to ignore. Instead of choosing to disregard the conventions of the Classical period completely, what Beethoven did here was to take the forms, structures and ideas developed in the late 18th century and early 19th century, stretching them to express something new and exciting.

One example of this is the way in which Beethoven uses the wind section of the orchestra to set the pace for those who follow. Previously, the likes of the clarinet, flute and oboe would have been used to provide some orchestral colour here and there – but they weren't the main instruments of musical expression. In the *'Eroica'*, though, we suddenly hear themes and melodies played by the wind section first – something that went on to become an entirely expected characteristic of Romantic music (take the clarinet in Rachmaninov's *Symphony No. 2*, for starters, or the flute in Debussy's *Prélude à l'après-midi d'un faune*).

As for Beethoven himself, the composer was clearly on a roll after the *'Eroica'*: the rest of the music he wrote in his so-called 'middle period' displayed a similar sense of vision, bravura and intensity. Listen to his output from that time and you regularly hear how he developed the use of extremes in volume, rhythm and harmony.

For more than two hundred years, the *'Eroica'* has continued to capture the imaginations of musicians and Beethoven's fellow composers. Wagner was fascinated by the piece, arguing that it explored the four phases of heroism: action, tragedy, serenity and love. As a line in the sand, it marks the point at which Romanticism was born. After the *'Eroica'* was written, classical music could never be the same again.

PUTTING ON A SHOW:
THE FOUNDING OF THE ROYAL
PHILHARMONIC SOCIETY

'**A**djective. Devoted to music; music-loving.' So goes the dictionary definition of the word 'philharmonic' and, since its launch in London in 1813, the Royal Philharmonic Society has been dedicated to the classical music cause right around the world. Without its creation, we might well never have heard Beethoven's mighty *Symphony No. 9* (*'Choral'*), for reasons we'll explain shortly.

Nowadays, England's capital city has an array of orchestral riches to its name. There's the London Symphony Orchestra (Classic FM's Orchestra in the City of London) at the Barbican; the London Philharmonic Orchestra, meanwhile, is resident at the Southbank Centre. That's where the Philharmonia Orchestra (Classic FM's Orchestra on Tour) also performs on a regular basis, as does the Orchestra of the Age of Enlightenment. Travel around the city, and you'll find all sorts of other orchestras – from the London Chamber Orchestra and Royal Philharmonic Orchestra at Cadogan Hall, to the Academy of St Martin in the Fields just across the road from Classic FM's studios in Leicester Square. But in 1813, London could not claim a single permanent symphony orchestra to its name. Those ensembles that did perform tended to steer clear of large-scale symphonies and concertos – probably due in large part to the cost of putting these concerts on – and instead focused on smaller-scale concerts and events. So, despite being home to some of the world's most illustrious composers and musicians over the centuries, there was a desperate need for the city to have an established, credible concert series. Out of this predicament, the Royal Philharmonic Society was born.

Just over two hundred years ago, on a cold winter's night in January 1813, a group of music lovers gathered to form what would go on to become one of the most important organisations in the history of classical music. They declared that the Philharmonic Society would 'encourage an appreciation by the public in the art of music' by promoting 'the performance, in the most perfect manner possible, of the best and most approved instrumental music'.

Almost immediately, the organisation had a seismic impact on the classical music scene. Within two years, the acclaimed Italian composer Luigi Cherubini had been commissioned to write a new symphony, which was premiered by the Society in 1815. The following year, Beethoven's *Symphony No. 5* was given its UK premiere thanks to the support of the Royal Philharmonic Society. In 1817, exactly the same thing happened with his *Symphony No. 7*. By this point, the Society had formed a strong affinity with Beethoven, so in 1822 the composer happily accepted its offer of £50 to commission a brand new symphony – his Ninth. Beethoven took a while to deliver (seven years, in fact) but the work has since been described as the greatest symphony ever written – so, arguably a very good use of that £50.

Since its formation, the Royal Philharmonic Society has always been dedicated to the commissioning of new music, but, as is evident in the case of Beethoven, its members have also been keen to provide a vehicle for other pieces to receive their UK premiere. During the 19th and 20th centuries, the Society funded the first British performances of works by a huge number of composers, from Dvořák and Elgar to Mendelssohn and Vaughan Williams. By the turn of the 20th century, the Royal Philharmonic Society was really into its stride; nevertheless, in 1904, England was famously dubbed *Das Land ohne Musik* ('The land without music') by a prominent German critic, who reflected a view held by many that England had not seen a truly great composer of its own since the days of Henry Purcell in Baroque times.

It's therefore been crucial that the Society hasn't just provided an avenue for the British premieres of music from across Europe, but has also been at the forefront of commissioning new works from these shores. Contemporary composers such as Harrison Birtwistle and Judith Weir have been commissioned by the Society, and up-and-coming young British composers have also been supported, including Anna Meredith and Charlotte Bray. In 2013, the Society announced the launch of a series of 'mini-commissions' for composers aged under 25 – with musicians encouraged to submit a range of different works, from piano miniatures to a brass fanfare.

When the Royal Philharmonic Society began, it filled a much needed hole by creating a permanent concert series in London. Today, though, the work of the Society is far broader: it is central to cultural life in the UK, and plays a key role in promoting debate and discussion about music and the wider arts. Together with Classic FM, in 2009, the Society launched National Listening Day – a project that encourages listeners young and old to 'lend us your ears' so that music can be heard in a fresh way. The first National Listening Day took place as part of a two-year Classic FM-funded project called *Hear Here!* More than 78,000 people came into contact with the programme through more than 200 live events across the UK that dealt with everything from the history of classical music to the science of how we physically listen to the sounds around us.

As an historic organisation, the Royal Philharmonic Society will forever be remembered for commissioning Beethoven's *Symphony No. 9* (as well as much more music besides: Holst's *The Planets* and Mendelssohn's *'Italian' Symphony*, for starters). But, crucially, it is also a thriving charity to this day, constantly seeking to engage new audiences for classical music while at the same time refusing to be distracted from promoting the highest possible quality of composition and performance. Its current chairman, John Gilhooly, describes the Society as 'the conscience of the classical music industry'. It is certainly true that without it, the classical music world would be a much poorer place.

BEATING TIME: THE BATON AND THE CONDUCTOR

History is a little hazy on the precise date. It possibly happened on 10 April, or it could maybe have been on 8 May. Either way, the year was most definitely 1820, and the man on the podium at the Philharmonic Society's concert in London was one Louis Spohr. The matter in question was the decision by Spohr to use for the very first time what we now know as the conductor's baton.

Nowadays, it would be fair to assume that musical history has always had a place for the conductor, but the phenomenon of someone standing in front of an orchestra waving his or her arms about to keep time, without actually playing an instrument, has been in existence for less than two hundred years.

Up until the 1800s, performances of symphonies, concertos and the like had, in effect, been led by committee. Instead of having one person in charge at the front, control would have been divided between someone seated at the keyboard – regardless of whether or not a keyboard was being used in the piece of music – and the principal violinist as leader of the orchestra. Admittedly, there had been precursors to the baton: everything from rolled-up newspapers to violin bows, via large, cumbersome sticks and even a golden staff way back in 709 BC. But, nevertheless, 1820 marked a definite turning point in the history of music.

The reason for the confusion over exactly when a conductor's baton was first used stems from the fact that Louis Spohr's own autobiography is rather unreliable. It was written well over two decades after the year in question and Spohr was advanced in years and rather forgetful by this point. Although he confidently states that he conducted with a baton in April 1820, there are no conclusive contemporary accounts to back this up. On the contrary, it wasn't until a year later that the use of the baton became an accepted part of the London concert scene. Nevertheless, many scholars are content to accept that it was on 8 May 1820 that the practice occurred for the very first time, with Spohr at the helm.

Throughout the course of history, some of the world's most famous conductors have made very specific demands about the batons they wanted to use. Henry Wood requested one of over half a metre in length, while Arturo Toscanini always demanded a tiny stick weighing only three-quarters of an ounce. Mysteriously, Toscanini also always requested that a little green dot be painted on the tip of the baton, above the handle. It puzzled many of the musicians he worked with and the maestro never explained the reason for it.

Even today, many conductors choose to dispense with a baton. This particular piece of wood or fibreglass is by no means an absolute essential. Pierre Boulez never uses one; and Leopold Stokowski thought the baton to be surplus to requirements. You may therefore wonder why the invention of an optional orchestral prop could possibly be seen as one of the 50 moments that rocked the classical music world. The answer? Well, the invention of the baton went hand in hand with the invention of the conductor as a classical music star. Up until that point, with directorial duties shared between different musicians, the only shining beacon on the stage was the soloist. From now on, though, the conductor began truly to take his or her place in the limelight.

In the couple of centuries since the invention of the baton, the cult of celebrity surrounding the person on the podium has developed in some remarkable ways. The likes of Spohr and Mendelssohn – both fine conductors as well as composers – very much saw themselves as being primarily there to beat time and keep everyone together. They did not consider it their job to impose an opinion as to how the music should be played. That all changed, though, with the arrival of Wagner on the musical scene. Here was a man who wasn't shy about sharing his views. He made very clear to his musicians what he thought they should be doing and, from the late 1800s onwards, this kind of behaviour from a conductor became both accepted and expected.

The role of the conductor really flourished during the 20th century. A wide range of musical personalities took the helm at various orchestras, bringing with them both flair and individuality on a scale never seen before. At the New York Philharmonic, Leonard Bernstein seemed to be acting out the music at times, with his exaggerated gestures, facial expressions and animated movements. Meanwhile, his counterpart at the Berlin Philharmonic, Herbert von Karajan, was the measure of restraint, with his rigid posture, understated air and suspicion of emotionalism.

Today, conductors such as Simon Rattle, Gustavo Dudamel, Marin Alsop, Valery Gergiev and Vasily Petrenko can fill a concert hall on the basis of their name alone being on the poster. Back in 1820, the idea that the person beating time could have attracted an audience would have been laughable. Two hundred years on from now, we can only hope that the phenomenon of conducting will have further developed to include a great many more women on the podium, as this is an overwhelmingly male-dominated area of classical music – something that undoubtedly needs to change.

REWRITING THE RULES:
THE '*TRISTAN* CHORD'

The music of Richard Wagner has always had a particularly powerful effect on people. He's the composer whose pull is so great that fans go on a kind of pilgrimage to Bayreuth to see the whole of his *Ring Cycle*; his fantastical themes and epic use of the orchestra were revolutionary; and, on the podium, he helped to shape the role of the conductor as we know it today. He was artistically and creatively brilliant but there is no doubt that Wagner was a deeply unpleasant human being who held views that are completely unacceptable in society today. He was an anti-Semitic racist, a serial philanderer, and he was prepared to lie, cheat and steal to get what he wanted. With his monstrous ego and vile temper, he was one of the least likeable composers in history.

Despite that, his influence on the world of classical music remains undimmed. Performances of new pieces by Wagner were the 19th-century equivalent of film premieres – all heightened anticipation and feverish excitement. Describing

Wagner's opera *Tannhäuser*, the French poet Charles Baudelaire exclaimed, 'Listening to this impassioned, despotic music, painted upon the depths of darkness, riven by dreams, it seems like the vertiginous imaginings of opium.' And the composer Gustav Mahler, who experienced *Parsifal* at the tender age of 23, didn't hold back either: 'I understood that the greatest and most painful revelation had just been made to me, and that I would carry it unspoiled for the rest of my life.' Not everyone was a fan, though. Rossini, for one, made several cutting comments about Wagner's music, including this classic: '*Lohengrin* cannot be appreciated at first hearing, and I do not intend to hear it a second time.'

But when it comes to the single moment when Wagner well and truly rocked the classical music world, it has to be during his groundbreaking opera *Tristan and Isolde*. It's not actually the entire opera that requires our focus; rather, it is one particular chord in the opening orchestral prelude. In 1865, an unsuspecting German public first heard that '*Tristan* Chord', as it came to be known. It caused an incredible stir at the time: this simply wasn't what music lovers expected to hear. It appeared to redefine the whole idea of harmony and, although all sorts of modern scholars have argued that the '*Tristan* Chord' actually harks back to music of the past, those who heard it in the 19th century believed it could herald the disintegration of classical music as they knew it.

The particular chord itself is made up of the notes F, B, D sharp and G sharp. All sorts of musicological analyses of these four notes exist – but, to be honest, the individual notes themselves are not the most interesting point here. Instead, what was revolutionary and deeply disorientating was the way in which they were used together, to create a hypnotic sound that scholars have been debating ever since. During the composition of *Tristan and Isolde*, Wagner seemed to know that he was writing something controversial. In a letter to Mathilde Wesendonck, a woman who might well have been his mistress, he exclaimed, 'This *Tristan* is turning into something terrible! . . . I fear the opera will be banned . . . only mediocre performances can save me! Perfectly good ones will be bound to drive people mad.'

Up to the point that Wagner composed *Tristan and Isolde*, classical music had been on an astonishing journey, from early Renaissance polyphony through to hour-long, expansive Romantic symphonies. But one rule had always remained pretty much constant: musical sounds should resolve satisfactorily. Tunes and phrases weren't left hanging; the melody would return 'home', and all would ultimately be well. The '*Tristan* Chord', however, does not function in this way. Where resolution is expected, we hear ambiguity. Sounds are left ringing in our ears – hanging, even – and this made listeners at the time feel both uneasy and expectant in equal measure. With the '*Tristan* Chord', Wagner had moved music on to another level. In the 20th century, composers began experimenting with abandoning conventional harmony altogether, and many people see the '*Tristan* Chord' as the moment that paved the way for such atonality and avant-garde sounds.

They say that imitation is the highest form of flattery – and we only have to look at how many other composers have quoted the '*Tristan* Chord' to realise its effect on musical history. It crops up in everything from the Gilbert and Sullivan opera *H.M.S. Pinafore* to Debussy's piano suite *Children's Corner*. It features as a piece of sampled music in the Radiohead song *'Idioteque'*, and some have even argued that you can hear it in the music of Ozzy Osbourne's band Black Sabbath. All proof, if it were needed, that the 'Tristan Chord' is as relevant and intriguing in the 21st century as it was on the night of the opera's premiere on 10 June 1865.

A NEW WORLD ORDER: IMPRESSIONISM AND CLASSICAL MUSIC

Pierre-Auguste Renoir's *Lady at the Piano* was one of the most beautiful and famous works of art to have been created in 19th-century France. Completed in 1876, this oil-on-canvas painting shows a young woman sitting serenely in front of a keyboard. Painted at around the time that Impressionism was emerging as a major movement in the art world, it demonstrates the main features of this new artistic school. The artist uses colour and light to create a mood, in the belief that these textures are more important than replicating a literal depiction of the scene.

At around the same time, the French composers Claude Debussy and Maurice Ravel were beginning to apply similar approaches to classical music. Just as visual art is best understood when seen, so music is most clearly comprehended when heard. Words alone don't really do Impressionism justice; to understand the new sound-world that was being created, have a listen to Debussy's *Prélude à l'après-midi d'un faune*. Then you will be able to hear for yourself how the composer used the full palette of the orchestra to convey hazy moods and pictures, rather than clear-cut melodies and ideas.

There were two controversies surrounding the dawn of this new kind of music: firstly, the apparent abandonment of traditional chords and harmonies, and, secondly, the very use of the term 'Impressionism' to describe what was going on. When it came to the music itself, the conservative French critics of the day could neither understand nor condone what they heard as the complete disregard for what had come before. For centuries, classical music had been centred on the idea that there were neat, logical chords – and that certain chords fitted together, while others could never be heard side by side. All of a sudden, composers such as Debussy and Ravel appeared to be revelling in the creation of a musical melting pot, where hitherto unimaginable harmonies were being blended left, right and centre. They were also choosing to eschew established structures, such as the symphony or the sonata, instead opting to compose stand-alone pieces with evocative titles. If that wasn't enough, entirely new techniques were required to perform this new music – extensive pedalling on the piano, for example. This created a sound that was alien to the classical music lovers of Paris at the time.

When it came to the question of what to call this new kind of music, many were keen to presume that the principles of painting could easily be transferred across to the audio world. 'Impressionism' seemed to sum up the sounds of these new pieces. However, despite being a leading light of the movement, Debussy was himself quick to pour scorn on this idea, complaining that 'What the imbeciles call "Impressionism" is a term that is as poorly used as possible, particularly by art critics.'

Some music historians believe that an obscure French-Italian composer by the name of Ernest Fanelli was the actual inventor of Impressionism in classical music. In 1912, his piece *Tableaux symphoniques*, which had lain dormant for the best part of 30 years, received its premiere, and its Impressionistic musical ideas predated Debussy's early works. Ravel apparently commented, 'Now we know where his [Debussy's] Impressionism comes from.' But, today, Debussy is generally seen as being the main exponent of these new musical ideas, even if there was a foretaste of them elsewhere.

The advent of Impressionism was important not just because of its influence in France but also because of the far-reaching implications it had on the entire European classical music scene. In 1907, Ralph Vaughan Williams took himself off to Paris to study with Maurice Ravel; the young British composer was rather amazed by the new sounds he encountered, and he declared himself to have been afflicted by 'a bad attack of French fever'. Bear in mind: Vaughan Williams had left for Paris with the old-school style of composition ringing in his ears. Having studied with the eminent Irish composer Charles Villiers Stanford at the Royal College of Music, he would have been accustomed to the strict structures of the British choral tradition, and would have likely had an encyclopedic knowledge of the works of Mozart and Beethoven. Describing Ravel as 'the man who is exactly what I'm looking for', Vaughan Williams felt liberated, and began to allow this new Impressionistic sound to flavour his own music from this point onwards. It wasn't just Vaughan Williams, though. The dreamy, picture-painting music of many of the other big-name composers of the time, from Delius to Dukas, could be traced back to the influence of Debussy's and Ravel's work.

As we have said many times before, the development of classical music is linear. So, the dawn of this new Impressionist music laid the foundations for an entirely more radical approach later on in the 20th century. By beginning to mould, reinterpret and even disregard the forms, structures and sounds of the past, Debussy and Ravel were paving the way for serialism (see Moment No. 26). This proved to be an entirely new and often even more shocking approach to composition, which would shake the very foundations of classical music to its core. Traditional chords, harmonies and tonality were irrevocably weakened by the Impressionists – making it all the more easy to redefine them entirely when the serialists rode into town a few decades later.

A MATTER OF RECORD:
THE INVENTION OF
THE GRAMOPHONE

Some of our *50 Moments that Rocked the Classical Music World* are undoubtedly bigger than others. All of them are significant in their own way, but one or two are definitely more at the cataclysmic end of the scale. This particular chapter features one of those moments that changed everything about classical music for all time. Not only that, but it created a whole new industry alongside that of the performers and the composers. It also made a lot of people a lot of money, in the process becoming a net contributor to the creation and presentation of music.

Flick back a few pages, or a few hundred years if we're talking in terms of time, and we could easily be discussing Tallis and Byrd and their exclusive contract to print music in England. It was undoubtedly a game-changer. In terms of scale, printed music might have been a big step forward for composers, but the effect that the ability to record the sounds musicians made had on classical music has arguably been the greater. It affected not only composers, but also performers. The advent of recorded music changed everything because, for the first time, international superstars could be created in every continent in the world without their having to leave the comfort of the recording studio.

In one of those bizarre twists that often come to pass in the world of inventions, the man who actually pioneered the recording of music isn't the person who is widely credited with being its inventor. In this instance, he has only himself to blame, as perhaps he might have spent a little longer thinking through the practicalities of how his creation might actually be used. The splendidly named Edouard-Léon Scott de Martinville, a French librarian who did a bit of inventing on the side, managed to make a recording of a song as it was being sung and, in 1857, he applied for a patent for a machine he called the 'phonautograph'.

The trouble was that Scott didn't actually set out to make a device that played back the sounds that he recorded in an audio format. Believe it or not, he never included the idea of playback anywhere in his patent application. Instead, he was trying to create a machine that would visually record speech onto paper. You might think that this had already been covered successfully with the invention of the alphabet, pens and ink, but Scott's idea was to make it all much easier, so that his machine operated as a kind of automatic shorthand-taker. A century and a half later, a group of boffins managed to play back some of the recordings that Scott had actually made on his phonautograph, but that he himself had never heard. These included a performance of *'Au clair de la lune'* made on 9 April, 1860 – probably the oldest existing recording of a song anywhere.

So the honours for creating a machine that both recorded and played back music and other sounds go to Thomas Edison. His 'phonograph' used two needles and tinfoil cylinders. The first needle etched the sound onto the tinfoil and the second followed the etchings to allow the sound to be played back. The patent applications flowed thick and fast, with Alexander Graham Bell, Chichester Bell and Charles Tainter obtaining patents for a 'graphaphone'. Instead of tinfoil, this used slightly more hard-wearing wax cylinders. By 1887, Edison and the Columbia phonograph company were selling wax-cylinder recordings to the general public.

Next came the 'gramophone', with the inventor Emile Berliner jettisoning the wax cylinders in favour of flat discs. By 1909, Columbia had stopped making wax cylinders altogether, in favour of records.

Over the next quarter of a century, the recording innovations continued apace, with the German chemical company BASF producing thousands of metres of magnetic recording tape in 1934 to enable a series of major experiments into its use by Germany's AEG. (In case you've always wondered, BASF stands for 'Baden Aniline and Soda Factory'.) It wasn't until 1962 that the Dutch-based Philips invented the compact audio-cassette, and this gave music lovers a far more portable way of listening to their own choice of recorded music on the move.

Many of the companies that built the gramophone players also made the records to play on them. Decca,

EMI (Electric and Musical Industries), HMV (His Master's Voice) and the Gramophone Company itself were all intricately linked to the retail of what we would think of today in a computerised world as being both hardware and software. However, unlike Apple, which creates hardware (the iPod, iPhone and iPad) and also owns a major retail outlet (iTunes), these companies were actually creating the new recorded material themselves that they were then selling on to the general public to be played on their hardware. This enterprise spawned whole new industries. The Gramophone Company (eventually part of EMI), for example, invested in the now legendary Abbey Road recording studios in the St John's Wood area of North London. The first recording made there was by the London Symphony Orchestra under the baton of Edward Elgar, although later the studios became inextricably linked to the success of another EMI act, The Beatles. Abbey Road's Studio One remains a firm favourite for classical recordings today, although the studios now also have a fine heritage in rock and pop, as well as for recording major film soundtracks.

The advent of the compact disc and the digital download are moments in the history of classical music that deserve chapters all of their own, so we will come to them later. But it was the gramophone that started it all, allowing musicians to record musical performances for posterity and letting listeners build their own personal collections of their favourite recordings. It could be argued that this was one of the most truly democratising moments in classical music's history. As the number of different recordings of the great works grew, so people were able to contrast styles and performances in a way that had been impossible to do previously. Before the arrival of the gramophone, the only way of judging a particular work was to hear it live in the concert hall. The fortunes of the classical record industry have ebbed and flowed since the invention of the gramophone, but there is no doubt whatsoever that its arrival changed the face of classical music for ever.

MUSICAL NUMBERS:
THE ADVENT OF SERIALISM

Since the days of the Renaissance, classical music has travelled on an extraordinary journey, which has taken in the invention of new styles of composition, new musical forms, and entirely new instruments. Some changes have been welcomed with open arms: who could object to the flowering of the Romantic period, for example, with its beautiful melodies and heartfelt musical expression? Other developments, meanwhile, have been highly controversial, none more so than the advent in the early part of the 20th century of what came to be known as serialism.

By the 1920s, some influential classical musicians believed that the potential of tonal classical music (in other words, music based on the relationships of the notes of the diatonic scale, e.g. the white notes on the piano that give us the key of C major) had been exhausted. They felt that an entirely new approach to composition was needed.

The prime mover in this area of musical thought was the Austrian composer Arnold Schoenberg, who in 1921 invented a 'twelve-tone' technique of writing music.

Now, a subject like this risks veering into all sorts of technical language, accessible only to those who already know the classical music lingo. But, essentially, Schoenberg's style of composing disregarded the standard 'doh-ray-mi' musical scale, on which all Western classical music was founded. Instead, he invented an entirely new scale based on all 12 possible pitches (i.e. not just the white piano notes of C major but the black notes as well); these different 'tones' or notes were then put together in a mathematical way. The result was music that didn't have an immediate melody or 'hook' because there was no recognisable relationship between the various 'tones'. It was deeply disconcerting for a great many listeners, but incredibly exciting for those who wanted to see classical music embrace something new and be genuinely innovative. For listeners who were tired of what was known as 'functional tonality' the system now being pioneered by Schoenberg was one that they welcomed with open arms.

Twelve-tone music was quickly developed by many of Schoenberg's contemporaries, the most famous being Alban Berg and Anton Webern. So Schoenberg's version became just one part of this new approach known as 'serialism'. Pierre Boulez, who is still composing today, used serialist ideas extensively in his music, principally because of his long-held beliefs about how classical music needed to develop in the 20th century. As a post-war student in Paris, Boulez had booed Stravinsky as he walked to the podium to conduct the premiere of his *Four Norwegian Moods* and *Danses concertantes*, both of which Stravinsky composed during exile in America. Although a fan of the Russian's avant-garde works, Boulez believed, along with a great many of his contemporaries, that the musical Establishment of the time lionised composers who wrote tonal, 'Neoclassical' pieces. These students fiercely protested because they passionately believed that now was the time to herald the arrival of some-thing entirely new. Later in his career, when he himself was a successful composer, Boulez seized his opportunity to do something about it.

As a result of the dawn of serialism, many composers were encouraged to write music in this emerging style. For some, this was entirely natural: the challenge of composing according to completely new rules was one they threw them-selves into. But for others, the job of writing music that was critically acclaimed became ever more difficult. Within the classical music elite, a view developed (still held in some circles today) that melody was somehow bad or backward-looking. The argument went something along the lines that the world had been blessed with enough nice tunes; now was the time to do something different. Consequently, compos-ers who chose to write within a broadly melodic soundscape were no longer seen as the darlings of the serious classical music world.

Very quickly, serialist composers began taking a twelve-tone approach with pretty much every aspect of music. After all, they reasoned, if you could apply a mathematical struc-ture to the pitch of the notes, why stop there? Why not try it with the length, the volume, and every other parameter of music and sound as we know it? Today, the movement's critics understandably argue that all this ends up removing the creativity from the music, forcing it to become some kind of mathematical equation. Yes, the music is very clever; yes, if you've studied the technique in advance, it can certainly illuminate the performance; and, yes, it's an interesting concept. But crucially, despite the beliefs of those at the time, serialism did not go on to replace tonality. On the contrary, the 20th century saw the composition of some of the most beautifully tuneful pieces in all of classical music, as well as the advent of whole new genres, such as film soundtracks, that provided a perfect excuse for melody to thrive.

Serialism rocked the classical music world and provided totally new thinking when it came to what composition should be about. It was a radical departure from the prevailing way of thinking, and it excited a great many people who were already in the classical music club. Outside of that coterie, though, tonal music remained in demand. For all that serialism caused a fuss at the time, a century later it's clear that, in the long term, melody remains king.

WE PREDICT A RIOT:
STRAVINSKY'S *THE RITE OF SPRING*

I f you happened to see the brilliant TV drama *Riot at the Rite*, starring Griff Rhys Jones, you will know something of this extraordinary story already. On 29 May 1913, the Théâtre Champs-Elysées in Paris was the venue for the premiere of Igor Stravinsky's ballet *The Rite of Spring*. What ensued that night has since become one of the most famous and controversial moments in the history of classical music.

On the evening in question, the audience was packed with the early 20th century's biggest names when it came to French artists and intelligentsia. Picasso was there, as were Cocteau and Proust; famous composers including Debussy and Ravel were also in attendance. It was the hottest ticket in town and all of Paris high society had come out to play. With music by Stravinsky and choreography by the acclaimed Russian ballet dancer Vaslav Nijinsky, everyone reckoned that the new ballet was bound to be good, but nobody in the

Parisian audience could have predicted what actually happened once the music began.

It would be fair to say that everyone in the audience was well aware that *The Rite of Spring* was not going to share the same saccharine innocence of a ballet such as Tchaikovsky's *The Nutcracker*. Nevertheless, to find themselves suddenly experiencing a work that dealt with the pagan sacrifice of a young virgin was clearly too much for many in the auditorium. These people were used to ballets that extolled grace and poise; instead, the dancers stamped their feet as their bodies convulsed. As one of the ballerinas later said, 'With every leap we landed heavily enough to jar every organ in us.'

After their initial bewilderment, the response from a large section of the audience was to boo, cat-call and shout their disapproval. The primeval rhythms and dissonant music, combined with angular dancing and pagan themes, caused outrage. As the conservatives booed, the progressives fought back – after all, there were plenty of people there who delighted in such adventurous and risky art. Physical fights broke out between opposing members of the audience and, in a desperate attempt to control things, the theatre's owner started turning the lights on and off in quick succession. Quite how he expected this to calm things down is something of a mystery, when it can have served only to inflame the proceedings further.

All the while, the musicians continued to play and the dancers continued to dance. The theatre had been on the warm side at the start of the evening – but by this point, it was absolutely boiling, which surely went some way towards fuelling the intense atmosphere inside. It wasn't even as if

Stravinsky had lulled them into a false sense of security: from the very opening of the piece, things were completely unpredictable. *The Rite of Spring* begins with a solo bassoon (unusual in itself) playing a disconcerting, earthy and seemingly formless melody. Within seconds, jarring, piercing chords, played in an entirely alien rhythm, come storming in from the strings. After barely a few seconds have passed, Stravinsky has created an unconventional, dark and menacing world, cutting through everyone's perceptions of what the beginning of a ballet conventionally sounds like.

By the time the interval was eventually reached, the police had arrived to attempt to restore order. But this they never managed to do. After a brief period of calm, the second act began – and, like moths to a flame, the incensed audience began to express its outrage in ever more extreme ways. A full-scale riot was perilously close to breaking out; Stravinsky was so concerned for his own safety that he left the theatre before the premiere had finished.

Part of the reason for the outrage was perhaps because Stravinsky had chosen to use the medium of ballet for this new music. Ballet was an art form known for its harmlessness and purity, with dancers who succeeded precisely because they looked younger than their years. Even in cosmopolitan Paris, audiences were used to ballet usually being wholesome, innocent, and decidedly sugar-coated. In an instant, Stravinsky had taken something hallowed and turned it into a grotesque version of itself. The way in which a pastoral theme was twisted in *The Rite of Spring* should also not be underestimated. Before this point, spring had been represented in music through works such as Beethoven's joy-filled *'Pastoral' Symphony* or Schumann's ebullient *'Spring' Symphony*. Here, by extreme contrast, Stravinsky painted a musical picture of a girl dancing herself to death, to bring about the start of the season.

Today, *The Rite of Spring* is acknowledged as one of classical music's greatest masterpieces. Stravinsky's use of the full colour of the orchestra to mesmerising effect, and the way in which he collaborated with Nijinsky, has rightly resulted in it becoming one of the most enduring and popular ballets in the world. It also serves as a powerful reminder of how political music can be: although Stravinsky might not have foreseen that he would have a riot on his hands, he must surely have known that he was making a bold and controversial statement here, bringing pagan themes into the mainstream. Musical norms had been well and truly pulled apart and thrown into the air, to the delight of some, and the outrage of many.

In the century since its premiere, *The Rite of Spring* has appeared in the Disney film *Fantasia* and has been cited by many famous composers as an inspiration – including the film music legends John Williams and Jerry Goldsmith. Aaron Copland thought *The Rite of Spring* to be a masterpiece: he was heavily inspired by the way in which Stravinsky had structured the work. And Leonard Bernstein summed up *The Rite of Spring* by saying it contained 'the best dissonances anyone ever wrote'.

A hundred years on, Stravinsky's thrilling ballet remains visceral, exciting and controversial. In 1913, it didn't just rock the classical music world: it shook its very foundations.

THE LURE OF THE SILVER SCREEN: THE FIRST FILM SOUNDTRACK

The first film soundtrack might have accompanied a movie that lasted for only around a quarter of an hour, but in 1908 a film of that duration was actually longer than usual. *L'Assassinat du duc de Guise* told the story of how the French King Henri III murdered his rival Duke Henri de Guise back in 1588. Although the film was critically well received at the time and remains of interest to cinema historians, in itself it is unlikely to be a box-office hit again any time soon. So, it is for being the first film with its very own soundtrack that it will chiefly be remembered. Camille Saint-Saëns was one of the most famous French composers of the time and a big name in creating work for the theatre. He wrote the score when he was in his seventies, working on the music scene by scene in front of a projection of the film. Initially, the music was for orchestra, but he later created a version that enabled a pianist to play along.

Saint-Saëns is by no means the only serious classical

composer to have dabbled in the cinema. He was at the vanguard of a long list of mainstream classical composers who have written specifically for the silver screen, including Malcolm Arnold, Benjamin Britten, Aaron Copland, Philip Glass, Aram Khachaturian, Eric Korngold, Sergey Prokofiev, Dmitri Shostakovich, Ralph Vaughan Williams and William Walton. The link between film soundtracks and core classical music is unarguable – in many ways, it is the natural development of the long tradition of composers writing incidental music to be used during performances of stage plays. Examples of this include Beethoven's *Egmont*, Mendelssohn's *A Midsummer Night's Dream* and Grieg's *Peer Gynt*.

Not all of the music used in the cinema was composed specifically for that purpose. Film directors have been quite happy through the years to appropriate existing classical works, often from long-dead composers, when they believe that an existing classical hit would do the job better than a newly commissioned score. Sometimes, this can bring a long-forgotten piece of classical music back into the listening public's consciousness. Some of the most famous examples of works from the core classical repertoire being given a new lease of life as a celluloid accompaniment include Rachmaninov's *Piano Concerto No. 2*, which features in *Brief Encounter*; Mozart's *Clarinet Concerto* in *Out of Africa*; and Richard Strauss's *Also Sprach Zarathustra* in *2001: A Space Odyssey*. Believe it or not, Mozart's *Eine kleine Nachtmusik* even made an appearance in *Ace Ventura: Pet Detective*, of all places.

None of these works can truly be said to be film soundtracks though, so they don't really follow on from the pioneering score written by Saint-Saëns. There are plenty of composers who have made their names writing specifically for the big screen. Richard Addinsell penned the *Warsaw Concerto* as a pastiche of a Romantic piano concerto for the 1941 film *Dangerous Moonlight*, as well as the scores for *Goodbye Mr Chips* and *The Prince and the Showgirl*. The Italian Ennio Morricone began his professional life playing in a jazz band, but ended up scoring films ranging from *The Mission* to *The Good, the Bad and the Ugly*. Yorkshire-born John Barry inherited his love of films from his father, who was a cinema projectionist. His big hits include *Dances with Wolves*, *Born Free* and *Out of Africa*.

Elmer Bernstein was one of the heavyweights of the soundtrack world, penning such delights as the music to *The Magnificent Seven*, while Max Steiner wrote the theme for *Gone with the Wind*. And then there was Eric Coates, who gave us *The Dambusters March* – a work that, in fact, he had already written before the film came along. He just needed somewhere to put it. Jerry Goldsmith was another of the giants of the film-music world, his scores ranging from *Star Trek* to *The Omen*. In terms of scary soundtracks, it would be impossible to miss out Bernard Herrmann and the music to *Psycho* from any comprehensive list.

The undoubted king of the living film composers, John Williams, has written the music for more than a hundred different movies and has garnered a mantelpiece-busting amount of critical acclaim along the way: he has 48 Oscar nominations (the highest number for any living person), carrying off the statuette five times. He has been nominated for 24 Golden Globes, winning four times. Of his 59 Grammy Award nominations, he has been victorious on 21 occasions.

In 1973, he met the director Steven Spielberg, with whom he has subsequently enjoyed the greatest creative partnership of his long career. Their first film was called *Sugarland Express*. Since then, their list of credits includes blockbuster after blockbuster. Williams also collaborated very successfully with the *Star Wars* director, George Lucas, working on all six films in the series. He also has a very special relationship with the London Symphony Orchestra, which has long been his ensemble of choice for many of his biggest projects. Williams's soundtracks include *Schindler's List*, *Harry Potter*, *Superman*, *E.T.*, *Jaws*, *War Horse* and *Lincoln*.

The big international names in film composing right now include Canada's Howard Shore (*The Lord of the Rings* and *The Hobbit* trilogies); the USA's James Horner (*Braveheart* and *Titanic*); Germany's Hans Zimmer (*Gladiator*, *Rain Man* and *The Lion King*); and fellow German Klaus Badelt (*Pirates of the Caribbean*). Craig Armstrong (*Romeo and Juliet*) and Patrick Doyle (*Sense and Sensibility*) are among Scotland's most successful film composers. England offers Nigel Hess (*Ladies in Lavender*), Rachel Portman (*Chocolat*), Stephen Warbeck (*Shakespeare in Love*), Howard Goodall (*Mr Bean*) and Debbie Wiseman (*Wilde*).

Writing for the cinema is big business and it's music that is widely heard, but some people argue that it should not be considered as part of classical music. We beg to differ. With a pedigree that stretches back more than a century to that initial 15-minute score by Saint-Saëns, we firmly believe that much of the music written for the movies today will remain among the most often heard and performed contemporary symphonic works for decades to come.

29

A NEW POLISH: 'FURNITURE MUSIC'

'There is a need to create furniture music: that is to say, music that would be a part of the surrounding noises and that would take them into account.' So wrote the French composer Erik Satie in early 20th-century Paris, after spending an afternoon having lunch with his friend, the artist Fernand Léger. Satie believed that this music would perform a very particular purpose in hiding the everyday noises of dining in a busy urban setting.

This could mark the first time a composer positively welcomed the idea of 'background music' – at least since the 16th century and *Tafelmusik* or *Musique de table*, which was intended as an aural complement to feasts and banquets. Here, Satie was not just accepting, but actually endorsing, the fact that music could be used as an accompaniment to doing something else. This paved the way for an army of imitators during the course of the century that followed.

Erik Satie was admittedly the most eccentric composer

of the early 20th century: his collection of silk handkerchiefs was legendary, and his frankly bizarre titles for pieces of music (*Three Flabby Preludes for a Dog* being an apt case in point) demonstrate his unusual nature well. After all, it's not without good reason that the humorist and close friend of Satie, Alphonse Allais, once gave him the nickname Esotérik Satie. But that doesn't mean his idea for furniture music should be dismissed. Once you strip away the quirkiness, there lies within a clever and thought-provoking suggestion about how classical music could or should relate to life in general.

Shortly after espousing his theory for the first time, Satie fleshed out the notion of furniture music to his friend Jean Cocteau: '*Musique d'ameublement* – Furniture Music – for law offices, banks, etc. . . . No marriage ceremony without furniture music . . . do not enter a house which does not have furniture music.'

It was a bold and extreme vision, but Satie was making the point that classical music should not necessarily be restricted to the concert hall alone. On the contrary, what is inherently wrong about a composer writing music to be used as the background to something else? Satie himself composed various pieces for use as furniture music: during his lifetime, one of the most successful was a set of short works, all of which took melodies by other well-known French composers, including Camille Saint-Saëns, and reworked them in a new way. These pieces were designed to be heard during the intermission of a Parisian play in 1920, with the audience being encouraged to take a look at a selection of children's drawings while letting the music wash over them. But, in practice, many of the assembled crowd instead stopped to listen to the live musicians, much to the consternation of the composer, who insisted they talk, mingle and discuss the art in front of them rather than pause to take the music on board.

Around the turn of the century, Satie had built up a great deal of experience as a cabaret pianist in Paris. It was while undertaking this role that he first met fellow French composer, Claude Debussy. By the time the term furniture music was coined, Satie had already gained a thorough understanding of how music could be used as an effective accompaniment to something else. As he once commented, 'There is no need for the orchestra to grimace when a character comes on stage . . . what we have to do is create musical scenery . . . in which the characters move and talk.' This same principle was applied to furniture music. It was Satie's vision that every social situation, no matter how large or small, would include some kind of discreetly played music, cushioning any awkward moments and providing an ideal way of enhancing or altering the mood of the gathering in question.

Another way in which this most individual of composers was breaking new ground here was by making a very clear distinction between credible, serious 'art music' written for performance in the concert hall and the more run-of-the-mill, 'music to order' concept of furniture music. He never claimed that his proposal would lead to great, lasting works of art; on the contrary, he simply stated that 'Art . . . is something else.' Satie sought to prove that it was entirely possible for a composer to write stand-alone music that would be critically appreciated, as well as pen relatively trite but entirely appealing background melodies for use in the modern world.

At this point in history, classical music was still mainly a revered and protected art form, enjoyed by an artistic elite but not necessarily experienced by the average citizen. This was arguably the case to an even greater extent in Paris, where artists and musicians mixed in a hugely creative but relatively tight-knit circle, in which your average man or woman would probably not have been made to feel immediately at home. Satie's idea of furniture music would, he hoped, now see classical music being experienced in many different environments, in a way that connected with people's everyday lives. This is a concept we might take for granted today, but it was pretty unusual a hundred years ago.

By the time of his death in 1925, Erik Satie had made quite a mark in the classical music world. His beautiful *Gymnopédies* for solo piano remain hugely popular today, and with his innovative larger-scale orchestral pieces such as *Parade* and *Socrate* he made waves in Europe and beyond. If Satie were alive now, one could only wonder at the levels of his creative excitement at the use of sound in our modern world, with its on-hold telephone music, permanently ringing mobile phones and dubious panpipe melodies being played in department stores around the globe. Although there's much about the use of music in the modern world that might exasperate us at times, we should still thank Erik Satie for championing new ways in which music could be used in everyday life.

MAKING MONEY AND ALL THAT JAZZ: GEORGE GERSHWIN

Although he lived a relatively short life, George Gershwin was among the most commercially successful classical composers of all time, becoming the first musician to earn a million dollars from one piece of music alone.

The piece of music that proved to be dripping in royalty-cheque gold for the American was the song 'Swanee', penned when Gershwin was just 20 years old. By that stage, his musical talents were already being recognised. He was receiving $35 per week from the publishing company T. B. Harms, to whom he would grant the rights to any songs he composed in return for his regular pay cheque. The arrangement worked well for the publishers, too: within the first year, three entire Broadway shows were staged using material written by Gershwin.

With typical youthful abandonment, Gershwin claimed to have dashed off the tune for 'Swanee' in just a few minutes while travelling on a bus in Manhattan. It didn't matter though, because it set him on the path towards unimaginable riches, establishing him as one of the first 20th-century composers to make a fortune from his music. Written originally in 1919 for a New York revue show, 'Swanee' came to prominence only in the 1920s after it was recorded by the singer, comedian and actor Al Jolson. Two million copies of the record were sold, alongside a million copies of the sheet music. It remained at the top of the American charts for a solid nine weeks running.

All this success was, on one level, unsurprising. From a young age, Gershwin possessed admirable musical and financial nous. He left school at the age of sixteen and cut his teeth as a music 'plugger', working to gain exposure for publishers' latest musical offerings. His experience as a music industry insider enabled him to see precisely what kind of material was genuinely popular, giving him a crucial advantage when it came to composing a hit song of his own.

George Gershwin didn't only rock the musical world once with the success of 'Swanee', though. He went on to do it again, becoming the composer who introduced jazz to the concert hall with his hugely popular *Rhapsody in Blue*. While still working as a plugger, Gershwin had diligently continued with his classical music studies, spending six years learning about harmony and orchestration with the violinist and teacher Edward Kilenyi. Consequently, when international stardom and financial success came, Gershwin was already in a very good intellectual place from which he could firmly establish himself on the classical music scene.

Written originally for a jazz band and later arranged for piano and full orchestra, *Rhapsody in Blue* received its premiere on 12 February 1924. By this time, Gershwin's name was already very well known, with his songs 'Fascinating Rhythm' and 'Oh! Lady Be Good' having gained widespread popularity across the United States. On this particular February night, George Gershwin blended the musical worlds of jazz and classical to such acclaim, in a way never accomplished before, that his name would undoubtedly go down in history for yet another reason. It's worth remembering that in the high-end classical music circles of America, jazz wasn't just frowned on – it was seen as being utterly outrageous. This genre, so intimately associated with drinking and the Prohibition era (which had begun only in 1920), was now being heard in the concert hall for the very first time. But, far from being dismissed, Rhapsody in Blue caused delight and immediately became one of the most popular pieces of its day.

Hot on the heels of the success of Rhapsody in Blue, George Gershwin was inspired to compose an entire concerto for the piano, which he completed in 1925. The American public took both these works to their hearts but the acclaim for them spread further, too: within a few years, they were being regularly performed in the concert halls of Europe, and today, Rhapsody in Blue and the Concerto in F are regular entries in the Classic FM Hall of Fame, our Top 300 chart of the UK's most popular classical music.

The 1920s were an extraordinary time for George Gershwin. Barely out of his teens, he had made history with his get-rich-quick song 'Swanee' and, just a few years later, he was redefining the whole idea of what sort of music could be heard in the concert hall. He achieved both these feats with total success, instead of receiving the critical mauling that might have been expected. Gershwin's music was welcomed by an appreciative American public evidently only too aware of just how unbelievably talented this young musician was.

The following decade was to prove equally productive: spurred on by the acclaim he received, he delivered hit after hit, not least his wonderful orchestral poem *An American in Paris* and his jazz-infused *Preludes for Piano* which seem to pick up where *Rhapsody in Blue* left off.

Today, Gershwin is revered as one of America's finest and most influential composers. Posthumously awarded the Pulitzer Prize for Music in 1998, he remains one of the most important names in the history of classical music, not just for his groundbreaking financial success, but for his ability to show that 'crossover' is by no means a dirty word. He knew what his audience wanted: after completing his opera *Porgy and Bess* towards the end of his tragically short career, Gershwin himself commented, 'True music must repeat the thought and inspirations of the people and the time. My people are Americans and my time is today.' Arguably, Gershwin's time is still continuing right now, with his music remaining incredibly popular the world over.

BACK TO THE FUTURE: THE REDISCOVERY OF VIVALDI'S VIOLIN CONCERTOS

A long with Johann Sebastian Bach and George Frideric Handel, Antonio Vivaldi makes up the trio of the most famous composers of the Baroque period. Many people have encountered his music for the first time in the concert hall – but perhaps a great many more have discovered it while being told: 'Your call is very important to us, and an operator will be with you as soon as possible.' Vivaldi's ubiquitous set of concertos known as the *Four Seasons* has appeared on hundreds of telephone on-hold services the world over, as well as being put to use in countless TV advertisements – from Peugeot and Sky to Hewlett Packard and Saga.

These are by no means the only concertos Vivaldi composed for the violin, though; in fact, he wrote hundreds of concertos in the 18th century. What's more, a number of them lay dormant for the best part of two hundred years

– and their discovery by a musicological researcher in the 1920s was something of a classical music sensation.

It was in the autumn of 1926, to be precise, in a boarding school in the Piedmont region of Italy, where the manuscripts of numerous concertos were found. At that time, the school was rather hard up and in need of some additional income. The discovery of these potentially lucrative scores was an attractive proposition for the school's governing body. They hoped to sell them to a local antique dealer and so requested the help of the National Library of Turin to value the historic documents.

The man responsible for coming up with that magic number was Alberto Gentili, at that time the Professor of Music at the local university. On receipt of the documents, which were sent to him by the crate-load, Gentili quickly realised he was in possession of a potential goldmine. Manuscript after manuscript of music, all signed by Antonio Vivaldi himself, lay before him. Rather than aim to profit from the venture, Gentili took the noble approach of ensuring the greater good for the musical world at large. Quickly comprehending the value of the material, and the interest it would no doubt garner from abroad, the professor enquired as to whether Turin University could purchase the collection for safekeeping. Sadly, funds were not forthcoming; however, Gentili refused to give up, and he managed to track down a wealthy local man who was willing to buy the manuscripts and immediately donate them to the university in memory of his recently deceased son. For hundreds of years, they had lain undiscovered. Now, these pieces were about to begin a journey towards once again becoming well known – but this time the world over.

It's an oft-repeated truth that a great many classical composers were not properly appreciated in their own lifetimes. Bizet, for example, never lived to see the huge success that became of his opera *Carmen*. In the case of Vivaldi, it wasn't so much that he was snubbed in his own lifetime, but that he was dismissed barely a moment after he had died. Within months of Vivaldi's passing in 1741, his music was being discarded; critics and audiences thought it not worthy of attention and so, very quickly, a great many of his previously popular works disappeared into obscurity. Today, it's hard to imagine that these Baroque pieces truly came to light only in the 1920s – but in reality, they have been known in the classical world for less than a century.

The danger of the success of Vivaldi's music is that its ubiquity can lead people to tire of hearing it. His *Four Seasons*, the most recorded classical piece in history, is the most obvious case in point. But many of his concertos are, quite simply, masterpieces, and have formed the basis of several musicians' international fame over the last 30 years. Nigel Kennedy was a relatively unknown violinist until, in 1989, he released his groundbreaking recording of the *Four Seasons* with the English Chamber Orchestra. It was an astonishingly successful album, selling more than two million copies. At the very height of its success, the equivalent of one CD every 30 seconds was being sold in the UK.

In their day, many of Vivaldi's concertos were revolutionary in their own right. After all, here was one of the very first examples of 'programme music' (in other words, music composed specifically to tell a story or paint a picture). And since the 1930s, pretty much every famous violinist in the world has committed his music to disc, from Anne-Sophie Mutter's famously slow, Germanic recordings through to the sprightly, infectious playing of the Italian Baroque band Europa Galante with their leader and violin soloist Fabio Biondi. It is genuinely astonishing to think that without the discovery of those manuscripts in Piedmont less than a century ago, many of Vivaldi's concertos would be completely unknown.

SILENCE IS GOLDEN: JOHN CAGE'S *4'33"*

During the course of the 20th century, the world produced many fine pianists. But how many of us could genuinely say we're already well acquainted with the work of David Tudor? His is not a name that appears on the album sleeves of many classical music lovers' CD collections, yet Tudor played a vital role in bringing one of the most unusual and utterly unique pieces of music (if we can even call it that) to the concert hall stage for the very first time. On 29 August 1952, David Tudor sat down at a piano in New York and performed the world premiere of the composer John Cage's seminal piece *4'33"* ('four, thirty-three', as the composer himself pronounced it). The assembled audience would have already been relatively warm to the idea of modern music; after all, by attending that evening they were raising money for the Benefit Artists Welfare Fund, an organisation that waved the flag for contemporary art. And yet, none of them was quite prepared for what the piece of music they were about to hear would entail.

The most controversial aspect of *4'33"* is that it contains absolutely no music, as far as we would define that term. In other words, the soloist does not play a single note nor direct any other musicians to do so. On that balmy August night, Tudor strode forward, purposefully placed the music score on the piano, and sat down to perform. At the moment when the audience would expect him to place his fingers on the piano keyboard, Tudor instead removed a stopwatch from his pocket and began the timer. Although the audience would have been oblivious to this, the score actually explained that *4'33"* should have three separate and entirely silent movements or sections. And the total length of the piece? No prizes for guessing that it had to last for four minutes and thirty-three seconds.

In Cage's mind, the 'music' contained within *4'33"* emanated not from the grand piano on the stage. Instead, the muted mumblings of discontent and confusion from the audience would provide the only sounds required within the piece. The premiere was taking place in progressive, liberal New York, but even this forward-thinking audience was by no means ready to embrace John Cage's idea of what constituted a genuine work for the concert hall. Decades on, when reflecting back on that premiere, Cage commented, 'People began whispering to one another, and some people began to walk out. They didn't laugh – they were just irritated when they realised nothing was going to happen, and they haven't forgotten it 30 years later. They're still angry.'

The choice of venue for the premiere of 4'33" was an interesting one. Maverick Concert Hall, in the Woodstock district of New York, is located next to a forest – and, on this hot August evening, the doors remained open. As a result, the sounds of trees rustling in the wind and birds flying in the air punctuated the confused murmurs from the audience, to create a bizarre fusion of disparate noises. Although it's since gone down as one of the most unusual pieces to have been composed in the 20th century, at the time of the premiere of 4'33" very few people seemed to get the joke (if there was even a joke to get). Some members of the audience were dismayed. Quite understandably, they could not comprehend how this silent 'music' could ever be considered as a serious composition.

Cage, on the other hand, refuted any suggestion that he had written silence. On the contrary, the very idea of the piece was that it would capture whatever noises those present at the time chose to make. The year before the premiere of 4'33", he had visited an anechoic chamber at Harvard University (this is a space where it is supposedly possible to encounter total silence). Cage, though, was sceptical of this idea: he believed he heard two sounds while in the chamber, and although those present attempted to explain them away, the composer remained unconvinced. In relation to the premiere of his new piece, Cage dismissed his critics:

They missed the point. There's no such thing as silence. What they thought was silence, because they didn't know how to listen, was full of accidental sounds. You could hear the wind stirring outside during the first movement. During the second, rain-drops began pattering the roof, and during the third the people themselves made all kinds of interesting sounds as they talked or walked out.

There are varying schools of thoughts about how *4'33"* should be seen within the context of classical music. For a great many people, the piece is nothing more than a cheap stunt and, given that no music is played, it should be considered as a passing moment of theatrical whimsy. Others, though, argue that, in writing this piece, Cage encouraged us to think more deeply about what we mean by the description of 'music', and how we all play a part in creating the sounds around us. Whichever view you take, the piece has remained an essential part of the music curriculum, with students all around the world being taught about the work in the half-century since its premiere. And in 2010, an online campaign was launched to try to get the piece to Number 1 in the Christmas charts. Although the perpetrators failed in their aim (the highest chart position in the Official UK Singles Chart for *4'33"* was Number 21), they did manage to amass 85,000 Facebook supporters for their cause – proof that John Cage's creation still has the power to inspire and, ironically, make a noise, more than 60 years after its premiere.

THE TV AGE:
LEONARD BERNSTEIN'S
YOUNG PEOPLE'S CONCERTS

On 18 January 1958, a telegram was sent to Leonard Bernstein from an unassuming address in New York. It contained just ten words: 'Incredible. Six year old chatter box entranced for solid hour.' The reason for this excited yet brief outburst was simple. On that same date, Bernstein had given his ever first televised New York Philharmonic Young People's Concert. On that particular occasion, the event was entitled 'What Does Music Mean?' Over the course of the next fourteen years, Bernstein would go on to present a great many more prime-time classical music television pro-grammes, all designed to introduce the genre to millions of viewers, especially the young, for the very first time.

In terms of revolutions in classical music broadcasting, Leonard Bernstein's Young People's Concerts were absolutely at the forefront of 20th-century efforts to democratise this great genre and make it accessible to anyone. There was no 'dumbing down' here, though: Bernstein's use of a full orchestra, and his choices of themes for each programme, ensured that every broadcast was presented with absolute credibility.

That first televised concert in January 1958 occurred just two weeks after Bernstein had been installed as the New York Philharmonic's new music director. There was already an education scheme in place when Bernstein arrived but he turned it into something with far greater impact, largely through his natural ability as a communicator to people who had previously not realised that they themselves might be classical music enthusiasts.

While Bernstein's conducting idiosyncrasies sometimes won him as many detractors as they did fans, no one could argue with his knack of being able to take a seemingly complex musical idea and make it completely comprehensible, even to a child. With such weighty topics as 'Musical Atoms: A Study of Intervals' and 'Folk Music in the Concert Hall', Bernstein set himself quite a challenge when it came to conveying the relevance of classical music to the American masses, but it was a challenge he evidently cherished, describing these programmes as 'among my favourite, most highly prized activities of my life'.

Originally, the Young People's Concerts were broadcast on Saturday mornings. Such was their success, however, that the CBS network then moved them to the ultra-primetime slot of 7.30 p.m. on Saturday evenings and, later, Sunday afternoons – proof that they were genuinely appealing to entire families, not just the young people for whom they were initially created. And it wasn't just American audiences who benefited from Bernstein's outstanding broadcasts: the programmes were syndicated to 40 other countries and were translated into many different languages.

The style of Bernstein's brilliant scripts was one of the main reasons for the huge success of the Young People's Concerts. They showed his desire to speak in a language young people would understand. He never, ever talked down to them, but nor did he insist on using overly technical terms simply for the sake of it. And Bernstein's choice of language was absolutely embedded in the culture of the day. Take, for example, his description of Berlioz's *Symphonie fantastique*: 'Pretty spooky stuff. And it's spooky because those sounds you're hearing come from the first psychedelic symphony in history, the first musical description ever made of a trip, written one hundred thirty-odd years before the Beatles.'

During the fourteen years the programmes were broadcast, praise for Bernstein's Young People's Concerts flooded in from grateful families across the United States. One eleven-year-old boy from Connecticut wrote saying, 'I guess I am just any boy who plays an instrument that wants to get all the praise for doing it nicely without practicing. I do practice but I do it more willingly after I watch your program.'

And this letter from a mother, kept today in the Berstein archives, typifies much of the correspondence Bernstein received:

> I want to say that after 30 years of enjoying music I, myself, now feel I know a bit more about why music is so enjoyable and I have grown to appreciate

modern American music – something a classically trained person sometimes struggles with. I am so thankful that my children – four of them – ranging in age from four to ten – can start their musical appreciation with such a *real*, *un-stereotyped*, *imaginative* explanation of its value. I want to thank you, so very much for all that you are giving the American people – I am so thankful that there are people like you who will open your mind to the medium of television – and hope that we will be able to see more and more of you and your orchestra in the future.

The often frosty classical music critics were also united in their support for Bernstein. After the fourth broadcast, the *New York Morning Telegraph* declared, 'Leonard Bernstein explaining the meaning and composition of music on the air still remains one of the most dynamic and one of the most fascinating presentations to be found in all of TV.' The *Courier Express* wrote, 'His name is Leonard Bernstein and he has done more than any man in the serious music field to bring understanding to the masses through radio and television.' And the great American conductor and composer was also lauded by the *Washington Star*, whose writer, Jessie B. Solomon, certainly didn't hold back:

Programs of this caliber make a great contribution to American culture. With the development of a preponderance of such types of programs and with the diminishing of the gangster-murder thrillers that adulterate the ether, the metamorphosis of our youth from the chrysalis stage to that of full-grown maturity can be towards an era that can bring a new renaissance of civilisation to our Western world.

Ask anyone of the baby-boomer generation in America how they were introduced to classical music and the chances are that the majority of them will cite Leonard Bernstein in their answer. It was an astonishing achievement and, considering the other musical heights that Bernstein scaled during his remarkable career, it still ranks as the one of which he should have been most proud because of the amazing difference he made to so many young lives.

AFTER THIS BREAK: CLASSICAL MUSIC AND ADVERTISING

This is another of those moments that is hard to pin down precisely in terms of a day and a date. However, we have chosen to include it because of its importance in bringing classical music to a mass-market audience, who might otherwise not listen to the genre at all.

A big part of our jobs at Classic FM involves going out and meeting people to talk to them about classical music. Sometimes, we come across individuals who swear blind that they have never listened to any classical music whatsoever at any point in their lives, that they wouldn't recognise a piece of classical music under any circumstances and that they could never countenance ever actually liking or wanting to own a recording of a piece of classical music.

And then we usually trot out a list of pieces of music that are used in television advertising. This list needs to be tailored to the age of our target but, presuming that they are over 40, we might ask them if they recognise the music from the Hovis ads, as the Yorkshire lad walks up a cobbled street, or the one where an Old Spice-wearing surfer comes crashing through the waves. Then there is the series of ads for Hamlet cigars where a hapless victim lights up to a familiar musical refrain, no matter what mishap has befallen him. And who could forget the jolly ditty proclaiming that 'Everyone's a [Cadbury's] Fruit and Nut Case'?

'Of course,' invariably comes the response. 'All of those pieces of music are well known to everybody.' Sometimes, though, there is genuine surprise when we reveal exactly where each of the pieces of music is to be found in its original form. All of these commercials use classical music to underpin the visuals. In case you're wondering exactly what is used in each of the examples in the paragraph above, here are the answers.

The second movement of Dvořák's *Symphony No. 9* has nothing to do with bread-making or Yorkshire. It was in fact written as a response to Dvořák's move to the USA. Despite being heavily influenced by African-American spirituals, it will, for many people, always simply be known as 'the Hovis music'. The ubiquitous 1970s aftershave Old Spice used a piece of classical music that was written in the mid-1930s by the German composer Carl Orff. Entitled *'O fortuna'*, it forms part of his cantata *Carmina Burana* and is a setting of a 13th-century poem. The second movement of Johann Sebastian Bach's *Orchestral Suite No. 3* (better known as the *'Air on the G string'*) provides the accompaniment to the Hamlet cigar ads, which haven't been seen on British television since the ban on tobacco advertising, although this tune became synonymous with the line 'Happiness is a cigar called Hamlet.'

Finally, Cadbury's turned to Tchaikovsky and *'The Dance of the Sugar Plum Fairy'* from his ballet *The Nutcracker* to accompany the commercials for their Fruit and Nut chocolate bars, featuring a voiceover from the distinctly plummy tones of the comedy writer Frank Muir.

Sometimes, a piece of classical music has had a relationship with a particular brand that has lasted for decades and has often been difficult to shake off, such is the strength of the association between the piece of music and the advertiser in the collective public mind. Who would have thought that a couple of sopranos singing in French about jasmine and roses would be locked into the brand psyche of British Airways? But the *Flower Duet* from Delibes's opera *Lakmé* looks likely forever to be twinned with the airline and has often been used as background music in messages to flyers on board planes, as well as in more traditional radio and television advertising.

Occasionally, music by contemporary classical composers starts out its journey to infamy because of its use in a television commercial. The Australian composer Elena Kats-Chernin became well known in the UK only when her *Eliza's Aria* was used extensively in the Lloyds TSB 'For the Journey' campaign, while the Welsh composer Karl Jenkins developed his orchestral work *Palladio* from a tune that originally accompanied an advert for De Beers diamonds.

There seems to be no lessening in the appetite for advertisers to tick the classical box in their campaigns, despite a bewildering choice of different styles of music from which they can pick. One of the biggest television advertising events in the world happens annually in the USA, when 110 million people across the country tune in for the Super Bowl. In 2012, it is estimated that each commercial of 30 seconds in duration cost advertisers an average of $3.5 million. Many of the ads are specifically created for the game and it is interesting to note just how popular the use of classical music is still proving to be. In 2012, Toyota's ad featured Richard Strauss's *Also Sprach Zarathustra*, while Coca-Cola featured a troupe of animated polar bears ice skating to Beethoven's *Symphony No. 5*. The snack manufacturer Doritos turned to opera for two of its adverts, with the *Overture* to Rossini's *The Barber of Seville* and the aria *'La donna e mobile'* from Verdi's *Rigoletto* taking centre stage. Time Warner used a section of Johann Sebastian Bach's *Well-Tempered Clavier Book 1*, while the chain of electrical superstores, Best Buy, opted for music from the contemporary American composer Philip Glass and his chamber piece *Glassworks*.

Why, then, do advertisers choose classical music so often? There is a big school of academic research in this area that suggests that classical music affects a consumer's mood in a very positive way. However, there might well be a more persuasive economic argument. Music composed by the likes of Beethoven and Bach is no longer subject to performance payments to the composer, so an advertiser gets a great tune and doesn't have to pay the composer for it. When you're stumping up millions to film a TV commercial on a sunny beach in Barbados, saving on the music costs might just make the overall numbers add up.

RUSSIAN REVOLUTION: THE DEATH OF JOSEPH STALIN

On 26 January 1936, when the composer Dmitri Shostakovich was 29 years old, a performance of his opera *Lady Macbeth of the Mtsensk District* took place in Moscow. The opera had been premiered a couple of years previously and had already clocked up well over two hundred performances since then in the Soviet Union alone – not to mention the stagings in New York and London. So, what made this particular performance so special? In the audience was the Soviet dictator Joseph Stalin, and to say that Stalin was unimpressed with *Lady Macbeth* would be putting it very mildly.

The writer Mikhail Bulgakov, who was in the audience that night, described the atmosphere as follows:

[The conductor] furiously lifts his baton and the overture begins. In anticipation of a medal, and feeling the eyes of the leaders on him, Melik is in a frenzy, leaping about like an imp, chopping the air with his baton. After the overture, he sends a sidelong glance at the box, expecting applause – nothing. After the first act – the same thing, no impression at all.

The themes of passion, romance and scandal in *Lady Macbeth* were quickly seized on by Stalin: the state newspaper ran the headline 'Muddle Instead of Music' – at which point, Shostakovich knew he was in trouble. According to the article, which would have been written by Stalin's Communist Party apparatchiks, 'Singing is replaced by shrieking . . . The music grunts, moans, pants, and gasps, the better to depict the love scenes as naturally as possible. And "love" is smeared throughout the entire opera in the most vulgar form.' Almost overnight, Shostakovich's masterpiece disappeared without a trace. Having become one of the most popular operas of its day, it was now a victim of extreme censorship.

The effect of all this on the composer was immense: instead of being artistically free, he now feared that the music he wrote would be forever suffocated by the Soviet regime. He withdrew his near-complete *Symphony No. 4* entirely and even feared for his life. As with many artists living and working under Stalin's regime, Shostakovich existed under a constant political cloud – and it was one that wouldn't lift until the dictator's death in 1953. The *Lady Macbeth* incident plagued Shostakovich for many years: it was even claimed that, decades later, in a bizarre, quasi-superstitious act, he wore a plastic bag around his neck that bore the text 'Muddle Instead of Music'. His family feared that the pressure and outrage could even lead the composer to commit suicide.

As if the censorship of *Lady Macbeth* wasn't bad enough, the Communist Party under Stalin continued to pursue Shostakovich in the years that followed. In 1948, he topped a list of composers the regime disapproved of; as a result, he lost a valuable teaching position at the Moscow Conservatory. Although Shostakovich did write music throughout his life, it wasn't until Stalin's death that he felt completely free to do so without fear of condemnation.

At that point, everything changed – not just for Shostakovich, but for hundreds of other composers and artists who had also been suppressed or frightened by his cruel regime. Stalin passed away in March 1953 and just a few months later, Shostakovich premiered his *Symphony No. 10*. He hadn't composed a symphony for a full five years, and although there are many differing interpretations when it comes what the piece is all about, the most longstanding claim is that at least part of it is a direct depiction of life under Stalin. The piece includes a terrifying march, which sees the percussion and woodwind soloists play like musicians possessed: there are menacing military drums, crazed piccolos and feverish string passages. For those at the symphony's premiere, there could be no doubt what this music was portraying. It is not until the very end of this long symphony that the sound-world is a triumphant one, with all the instruments playing a unified, uplifting melody that strongly seems to suggest Moscow is a better place without Stalin at the helm.

Many musicians and scholars rightly point out that quite a lot of the themes in Shostakovich's *Symphony No. 10* were actually written before Stalin's death – and it's certainly true that a great many of the ideas in the piece were sketched out extensively in the late 1940s and early 1950s. Nevertheless, the death of Stalin surely spurred Shostakovich on to complete the symphony and to tinge it with plenty of references to the regime under which he had so personally suffered.

After the premiere of his *Symphony No. 10*, Shostakovich wasn't particularly keen to comment on the inspiration behind it. He somewhat light-heartedly said, 'Like my other works I wrote it very quickly. That is probably more of a defect than a virtue because there is much that cannot be done well when one works so fast.' What he did do, though, was to surge ahead and compose a glut of new pieces: clear proof that the composer felt wonderfully liberated after the death of the man who had oppressed him so much.

THE PIANIST WHO CONQUERED
RUSSIA: VAN CLIBURN

'I had only a few months to prepare for the Tchaikovsky competition. But, in a way, my whole life had been leading up to it.' So said the Texan pianist Van Cliburn about his victory at the first International Tchaikovsky Piano Competition in Moscow, in March 1958. This particular competition had it all: controversy, politics, drama, and a huge dose of unbelievable talent. It also went on to produce the first ever million-selling classical record – creating history and demonstrating that there was a huge international market for this kind of music.

To understand the significance of this competition, we first need to try to appreciate the context in which it was taking place. If you're old enough to remember the 1950s, take a moment to cast your mind back to the world at that time. The Cold War was at its height. In 1957, Nikita Khrushchev triumphantly declared 'We will bury you!' to the might of the West, and Communism was seen by many as the greatest threat to peace and stability on the planet. To say that relations between America and Russia were tense would be a model of understatement. In the autumn of 1957, the Soviets had launched Sputnik over the skies of America, and many people seriously believed that a full-scale nuclear war was dangerously close to becoming a reality. All of which makes the fact that a Texan won a piano competition in Moscow named after one of Russia's greatest composers simply remarkable.

The jurors tasked with picking a winner that year make the panel on *The X Factor* look decidedly B-list. The chairman was none other than Dmitri Shostakovich – heralded as Russia's finest living composer, and recognised as one of the most revered musicians in the world at that time. Alongside him were the great pianists Sviatoslav Richter and Emil Gilels, and the composers Arthur Bliss and Dmitri Kabalevsky. What a line-up. Bliss, a British composer, was the only non-Soviet member of the judging panel – and, given the animosity and tension between Russia and the West, it would have been fair to expect the competition to be something of a stitch-up. Surely, any decent Russian pianist who made the final would be a likely shoo-in as the winner?

The competition itself began in the March of 1958. A total of 50 performers took part, all of them required to perform concertos by Russia's two most famous composers: Tchaikovsky and Rachmaninov. One particular competitor immediately stood out. This Texan's physical presence was quite something: at well over six feet tall, he was one of the most imposing competitors. He comfortably cruised through to the final round, and was then required to perform in front of a large Russian audience. Bear in mind – many of those in attendance probably believed themselves to be in the presence of an enemy. Van Cliburn's nationality was hugely provocative in itself, and that was before he had even sat down in front of the keyboard. Performing Tchaikovsky's *Piano Concerto No. 1* and Rachmaninov's *Piano Concerto No. 3*, both of which the audience knew like the backs of their hands, Van Cliburn realised that he had to pull something amazing out of the hat. Never had he performed in front of such an exacting and suspicious audience – and if he was going to stand a chance of winning, his performance needed to rise above political issues, to communicate something stunning to the assembled Russians.

Van Cliburn's playing was, quite simply, electrifying. The audience went mad; they knew they were in the presence of a truly astonishing musician. At this point, all attention turned to the jury. On one level, it was a no-brainer: Van Cliburn was unambiguously the finest performer, as shown by the audience's reaction, and he simply had to be crowned the winner. On another, his American nationality was a huge disadvantage. A number of jurors had already chosen a Russian winner, one Lev Vlasenko, because they believed him to be the person Khrushchev would approve of. Consequently, some decidedly lukewarm scores started coming in for Van Cliburn. Sviatoslav Richter, smelling a rat, decided to redress the balance. He awarded Van Cliburn the full 25 marks out of 25, while giving a number of the other competitors a big fat zero.

Eventually, Khrushchev himself was consulted about who should be crowned the winner. He asked who the best performer was; the jury replied that it was, without a doubt, Van Cliburn. 'Well, in that case,' he replied, 'give him the prize!' This they duly did, and the 23-year-old pianist returned to the States to be given a hero's welcome. In New York, a ticker-tape parade heralded his arrival, and newspaper headlines proclaimed him to be 'the Texan who conquered Russia'. With such outstanding talent evidently having been discovered, what would Van Cliburn do next? The answer was to release the world's first million-selling classical recording, containing that very same Tchaikovsky concerto that blew the Soviet audience away in Moscow.

Teaming up with Kirill Kondrashin, the conductor who had been on the podium at the Tchaikovsky Competition, Van Cliburn created an outstanding record that proceeded to make him a household name – not just in America, but across the rest of the world, too. In an era when avant-garde serialism was all the rage in classical music, here was proof that a great recording of an established favourite could still sell by the bucket-load. Van Cliburn's reward, in addition to the huge amount of money he received, included the Presidential Medal of Freedom and being inducted into the American Classical Music Hall of Fame. His legacy was his own Van Cliburn International Piano Competition, started in 1962 and held every four years since, to help discover the next young musical star. It's produced some outstanding winners over the last half-century – but none of them can match the skill and triumph of the man who bears the competition's name.

CARTOON CLASSICS:
WALT DISNEY'S *FANTASIA*

I t definitely wouldn't be an exaggeration to say that Mickey
Mouse is one of the best-loved cartoon characters (in fact,
perhaps *the* best loved) in the history of animation. Millions
of children have been enchanted by his antics and, together
with Minnie, Goofy, Donald Duck and the rest of the gang,
Mickey has been one of the most enduring symbols of Walt
Disney's universal appeal over the last century. But back in
the 1930s, Mickey Mouse was by no means adored. In fact,
children had a fairly ambivalent attitude towards this little
creature – and Walt Disney wanted to do something about it.
The vehicle he created to make Mickey one of cinema's most
appreciated creations was *Fantasia*, a film that introduced
millions of people to classical music and powerfully demonstrated its relevance outside the concert hall.

In 1938, Disney took the first steps towards creating
Fantasia. His artistic partner for this exciting cinematic adven-
ture was Leopold Stokowski, the respected conductor of the

Philadelphia Orchestra. In Stokowski, Disney found a kindred spirit. According to the conductor, 'The beauty and inspiration of music must not be restricted to a privileged few but made available to every man, woman and child. That is why great music associated with motion pictures is so important, because motion pictures reach millions all over the world.'

This idea of marrying classical music with cinema was by no means new; in fact, Walt Disney himself had been experimenting with the idea for a number of years already, through his slapstick *Silly Symphonies*, which began in 1928. But the premiere of *Fantasia*, at the Broadway Theatre in New York on 13 November 1940, took this idea to a far more exciting level. Initially, the project had the rather uninspiring working title of *The Concert Feature*, but Disney enlisted the help of his colleagues in finding an alternative name. After receiving well over two thousand suggestions (the worst of which was surely *Highbrowski by Stokowski*) it was decided that *Fantasia* best summed up this collection of animations paired with famous pieces of classical music.

Initially, the success of *Fantasia* was muted. It might seem surprising to us today that it was not immediately shown in cinemas across America – but this was the very first film to be released in full stereo sound. The new system needed to bring Disney's cinematic creation to life in the theatre was both cumbersome and expensive; in fact, around 20 per cent of the movie's entire budget was spent on getting the sound just right, because Disney was adamant that audiences should be able to hear the music in all its multi-channel, stereo glory. As a result, *Fantasia* was a fairly exclusive affair at first: appearing in just 14 cinemas nationwide, the film had a sort of cult appeal rather than reaching a mass-market audience. Walt Disney himself was apparently disappointed by these early results: he didn't see *Fantasia* as an immediate success and decided it was probably not worth pursuing any more music-based feature films of this nature.

Over the next decade, though, more and more people encountered *Fantasia* for the first time. It appealed not just to children but to adults, too: bear in mind, this new way of listening to surround sound in the cinema was as exciting for many parents as it was for their offspring. Consequently, Walt Disney went on to say that '*Fantasia* is timeless. It may run 10, 20 or 30 years. It may run after I'm gone. *Fantasia* is an idea in itself. I can never build another *Fantasia*.' The way in which the film introduced classical music first to the great American public – and then to filmgoers around the globe – meant that it had a very real musical significance, as well as a visual one.

Prior to the premiere of *Fantasia*, many of the pieces used in the film were known only by those who were already familiar with classical music. But within a few years, works such as *The Sorcerer's Apprentice* by the little-known French composer Paul Dukas had taken on an entirely new life. Today, very few of us who have seen the film are able to hear that piece without our mind's eye catching a vision of Mickey Mouse with his wand and cape, conjuring up all sorts of mischief in time to the music.

In fact, the initial concept of *Fantasia* stemmed entirely from this piece. Together with Stokowski, Disney worked to imagine an animation that had no spoken dialogue and showcased his favourite character in all his glory. This was, essentially, Mickey's moment to shine, but after it appeared to be going so well, both men agreed it would be a good idea to add in some additional cartoons and find the appropriate music to match. Consequently, rarely heard works such as 'The Dance of the Hours' from the Italian composer Amilcare Ponchielli's opera La Gioconda became forever associated with dancing alligators and hippos, while already popular melodies from The Nutcracker by Tchaikovsky were the backdrop for everything from mushrooms to flowers.

Sixty years after the premiere of the original film, the Walt Disney Company released Fantasia 2000, this time featuring the Chicago Symphony Orchestra conducted by James Levine. The only segment that links both this film and the original is Mickey Mouse's antics during The Sorcerer's Apprentice. Rather than simply reimagining the first Fantasia, the team at Disney created entirely new animations, set to similarly popular pieces of classical music including Gershwin's Rhapsody in Blue, Elgar's Pomp and Circumstance Marches and Stravinsky's The Firebird.

Rewinding back to 1940, nobody knew how Fantasia would be received. The linking of feature-length animation and classical music in this way was entirely new, but if anyone was going to make it work, it would be Walt Disney. And, today, we can be left in no doubt that the master achieved his aims. His collaboration with Stokowski powerfully demonstrated how relevant classical music could be to popular culture. Music in the concert hall is wonderful; equally, there is something very special about being able to experience an orchestra in full surround sound in a local cinema, complete with comical sorcery from a mouse who, it turns out, did indeed go on to become an international treasure – something that pleased his creator very much.

LESS IS MORE: THE INTRODUCTION OF MINIMALISM

In July 1968, the British composer Michael Nyman – best known today for his soundtrack to the Jane Campion film *The Piano* – was the very first person to use the word 'minimalism' to describe a particular style of music. Since then, this simple, pared-back, and often captivatingly repetitive style has influenced not just mainstream classical music but film soundtracks, pop music, jazz and a whole lot more besides.

The music Nyman was referring to when he coined the term minimalism had actually been born on the west coast of America. In the early 1960s, composers such as Philip Glass and Steve Reich were experimenting with an entirely new approach to classical music, which consciously moved away from the very complex, very difficult pieces that were all the rage at the time. This music was largely tonal (in other words, it was melodic rather than dissonant) and its hypnotic, repetitive nature would soon become extremely popular – not just in America, but across much of the rest of the West, too.

Up until this point, the music of the 20th century had all been about trying to become more complex and to break free from the traditions of the likes of Mozart, Beethoven and Tchaikovsky. Some composers, such as Arnold Schoenberg and Pierre Boulez, were writing serialist music (see Moment No. 26), which saw melody abandoned altogether in favour of a mathematical formula for composition. But a group of American composers decided to go back to basics, adopting the age-old formula: rhythm + pitch = music. It may sound too simple – but, sometimes, the least complex ideas produce the most stunning outcomes.

The beauty of minimalism is that it started out as something so simple. In the most elaborate symphonies, it's easy to miss the best bits among all the action, but in the first minimalist pieces even the smallest change was of huge significance. Listen to Terry Riley's *In C* from 1964: it's not a symphony in C or a concerto in C, it's just *In C*, plain and simple. The music starts with only the note C, played over and over again in a steady rhythm. Once your ears are used to the hypnotic rhythm and pitch, any unexpected notes or rhythms jump out from the texture with a striking impact.

It's not just instrumental pitches that are used to dramatic effect. *It's Gonna Rain* by another key minimalist, Steve Reich, uses speech from a sermon and sets it on a loop. While it might be slightly odd hearing the same words over and over again (listening to 'it's gonna rain, it's gonna rain, it's gonna rain' can get a bit depressing), eventually your brain ignores the meaning and starts to become hypnotised by the pitch and rhythm of the text. Reich used speech again in his 1988 composition *Different Trains*, which sampled interviews with Americans and Europeans about the years before, during and after World War II. The speech-inspired melodies for a string quartet, accompanied by train sounds and chug-chugging rhythms recorded onto tape, make for a poignant musical journey. This is especially remarkable considering the simplicity of the music.

Composers such as Philip Glass took this minimalist formula and developed it to huge success. In the summer of 1976, he rocked the opera world with his minimalist masterpiece, *Einstein on the Beach*. Where previously one could argue that opera had been oversized and over-indulgent, Glass found a balance between innocence and boundary-breaking innovation with his exciting new sound-world. But if Glass's early operas, with their relentless, undulating rhythms, don't float your boat, there's plenty of modern minimalist music to explore. The Italian composer Ludovico Einaudi uses basic harmonies and repetitive tunes that gradually blossom into simple yet beautiful piano studies. The Estonian master of minimalism, Arvo Pärt, meanwhile, takes music back to basics in his breathtaking *Spiegel im Spiegel* ('Mirror in the Mirror'), which captures enough emotion in the opening three raindrop-like notes from the piano to break your heart, even before the violin line floats in over the top.

One of the main achievements of minimalism was that it made it acceptable to compose melodic music once again. That might sound like an exaggeration, but at the time this movement began it was genuinely not seen as very 'progressive' to write anything with a tune. Instead, very clever music, very difficult music, but ultimately music that was extremely challenging to listen to was all the rage, with composers retreating further into their own small club of like-minded people who all earnestly appreciated the music they wrote. When the likes of Philip Glass, John Adams and, here in the UK, Michael Nyman started writing this very simple music, which was the antithesis of the musical world around them, it gave people permission to break free from the shackles of all things atonal. Steve Reich once summed this up brilliantly, saying he wanted to write music that reflected 'the real context of tail fins, Chuck Berry, and millions of burgers sold' – in other words, music that chimed with real life, rather than connecting only with an artistic elite.

In the decades that followed, minimalism took hold in many ways. Mike Oldfield's chart-topping *Tubular Bells* is a classic example of minimalist music – and, in the 1990s, bands such as Radiohead used techniques that could be traced back to Glass, Riley and Co. Today, the term 'minimalism' isn't often used, arguably because it's become so mainstream it now longer needs to be defined as an 'ism'. But, back in the 1960s, this completely counter-cultural sound heralded a dramatic gearshift in the way people defined classical music. Without that group of like-minded composers in San Francisco, who wanted to find a way out of the harsh, atonal music of their contemporaries, classical music could well have sounded very different over the last 50 years.

HITTING THE RIGHT NOTE: THE 1980 INTERNATIONAL CHOPIN PIANO COMPETITION

Talent competitions of any kind are nearly always divisive. For every one who thinks the latest *Strictly Come Dancing* winner was clearly the best, there will be another who reckons that the runner-up was robbed. For every victor in the *Sports Personality of the Year* competition, there will be an athlete who silently wonders what else they could have done to warrant the top prize. In music contests, it's no different. What made the 1980 International Chopin Piano Competition unique, though, was the level of controversy and outrage the final decision invoked.

The origins of this particular competition, always held in Warsaw, can be traced all the way back to 1927. And since 1995, this prestigious contest has been held every five years. It is, without doubt, one of the most important piano competitions in the world: the list of previous jurors reads like a

Who's Who of classical music, with everyone from composers Witold Lutosławski, Emil von Sauer and Karol Szymanowski through to pianists Nelson Freire, Vladimir Ashkenazy and Arthur Rubinstein taking part on the panel. But it was the reaction of Martha Argerich, a judge at the 1980 event, that truly rocked the classical music world.

One of the competitors that year was a young Yugoslavian pianist by the name of Ivo Pogorelić. He was already an established name in musical circles, having won the Montreal International Piano Competition earlier that same year, as well as another prestigious accolade in Italy in 1978. The 22-year-old's performances in Warsaw certainly made a statement, so much so that Argerich immediately declared him to be a genius. His stage presence also set him apart from the other competitors. With his long, shaggy hair and theatrical gestures, he certainly wasn't your average concert pianist. Pogorelić played at lightning speed and with an astonishing technique and accuracy, made all the more remarkable by his young age. His interpretations of Chopin's music were also unique: some would say inspired; others would argue unnecessarily idiosyncratic. He tended to exaggerate the music – so, if the instruction from the composer was to play the piece quickly, he would practically break the musical speed limit.

Unfortunately for Pogorelić, the overwhelming opinion of the jury was that his quirky style had no place in this competition. He failed even to make the final, but one particular juror wasn't going to allow this to happen without making her feelings known. Martha Argerich was absolutely outraged. She believed this young man to be one of classical music's most exciting stars of the future, and yet here were the other members of the panel seemingly extinguishing his dream before it had even begun. Argerich walked out in protest at the jury's decision, and refused to play any further part in the competition. She went on to say that she felt ashamed to have even taken part in it in the first place.

Reflecting back on the event some years later in an interview with America's National Public Radio, Pogorelić explained how disillusioned the whole process had made him feel. 'In 1980, people wrongly interpreted my attitude and approach to Chopin's music,' he commented. 'I wanted a certain form of confrontation, to see to what degree the results of my searching and fascination would appeal to the public.' Given all the negative press the competition received, and the uncomfortable focus for Pogorelić personally, you would be forgiven for thinking that the whole sorry saga was a bitter blow for him. However, such an assessment couldn't be further from the truth. Far from being shunned by the classical music cognoscenti, Pogorelić immediately found himself in receipt of a lucrative recording contract. He made his debuts in London and New York in 1981 and, by 1982, was signed up as an exclusive artist with Deutsche Grammophon – among the most prestigious of all classical music record labels.

Throughout his career since then, Ivo Pogorelić's playing has remained divisive. His unusual interpretations have continued to be a hallmark of his style – and not everyone has been quick to embrace them. Anthony Tommasini of the *New York Times* described a 2006 Beethoven concert from Pogorelić as going from 'weirdly fascinating' to 'just plain weird', concluding his review with the question: 'Here is an immense talent gone tragically astray. What went wrong?' This particular concert occurred after the pianist had taken a ten-year break from concert performances in the mid-1990s; his return to the stage was less than triumphant, being summed up by Tommasini as 'incoherent and interpretively perverse'.

Interestingly, in 2010, history seemed to be repeating itself at the International Chopin Piano Competition. Once again, a young pianist wowed the crowds, and once again, the judges didn't seem to take him to their hearts. On this occasion, things were admittedly slightly different: the pianist in question, Ingolf Wunder, did come second in the competition overall, whereas Pogorelić had failed even to make it to the final. But, nevertheless, the young soloist whose name was on everyone's lips evidently didn't do enough to convince the judges that he should be crowned victorious. Once more, though, just as had happened 30 years earlier, Deutsche Grammophon decided to offer a recording contract to someone other than the competition's winner. And so, the following year, Ingolf Wunder released his first album with the label. It was, appropriately enough, an all-Chopin recital. Which inspires the question: in 2040, should we expect another controversy along these lines? Only time will tell.

THE MEDIUM IS THE MESSAGE: THE INVENTION OF THE COMPACT DISC

Technological development moves fast these days and there is no better example of this than the story of the compact disc. It arrived in a blaze of publicity in the 1980s and became the ubiquitous music-storage system of choice. In the process, sales of music on vinyl albums and audio cassettes were wiped out for all but a few die-hard aficionados. Now, just 30 years later, it is possible to imagine a future where CDs themselves become museum pieces, as the digital download begins to take precedence. More of that in Moment No. 48, because this chapter is an opportunity for these optical discs to shine.

The arrival of the CD was momentous for classical music, but arguably not as momentous as the invention of the gramophone around the turn of the 20th century. The CD didn't do anything different to the gramophone in terms of being a way of storing music. What it did do though, was offer far greater portability than a vinyl album, at a vastly improved sound quality to the audio cassette. That meant music lovers saw a reason to replace their collections of vinyl and cassette albums with brand new digital CDs. This, in turn, created a huge boom for the record industry, with their coffers flowing over as music buyers bought the same music they had bought before, only this time on CD. When it came to new recordings, customers were initially prepared to pay a premium for digital recordings, so it proved to be even more lucrative for the record industry.

Let's take a quick look at the numbers. In 1986, 137 million CDs were sold around the world, but by 1996 the annual global sales had rocketed to 2,162 million CDs. That market was valued at an eye-watering US$34.7 billion. And that's just the CDs themselves. On top of that, people bought brand new hi-fi systems on which to play their music at home, while brands such as Sony repeated the success they had enjoyed with the cassette-based Walkman, by creating personal CD players, which sported the instantly understood and much loved Walkman brand. The unlikeliest industries also benefited: there was a period in the 1990s when no self-respecting bachelor pad was without its floor-to-ceiling CD storage racks.

Although it took a while for the CD to break through into the consumer market, it was invented by the Dutch company Philips back in 1974. At around the same time, engineers at Sony were developing their version of a digital optical disc. The company's then president, Norio Ohga, was a massive supporter of the CD. He was also a great classical music fan and had been planning a career as an opera singer before taking up a role at Sony. It's said that he was absolutely insistent that CDs should be 4.8 inches in diameter, so that they could contain 75 minutes of music. And the reason for this? Beethoven's *Symphony No. 9* was one of his favourite pieces and he was adamant that the new format should be able to contain the whole symphony on a single disc. The relationship between classical music and the compact disc was cemented even further when Richard Strauss's *Alpine Symphony* was chosen to be the piece of music used to test the newly created discs.

So, how exactly does a compact disc work? Now, we are no scientists, so it will no doubt be a gross oversimplification to say that CDs operate using a laser, which shines onto the readable surface of the disc, reading minuscule bumps on a tiny single groove that radiates outwards from the centre of the disc, depending on how the light refracts. The data that is stored on these bumps is basically a series of digits, which represents the sound. When a CD is manufactured, the digits are placed onto the disc and a CD player takes that information and turns it back into a faithful representation of the original audio.

There were drawbacks to CDs – not least that scratches to the underside of a disc can render it unreadable by the laser. However, they were nowhere near as easy to damage as vinyl records and were also not subject to wear and tear from friction, which can afflict the cassette tape. In 1981, the CD was discussed on the television programme *Tomorrow's World*, where the presenter showed off the disc's alleged indestructibility by liberally spreading strawberry jam all over a Bee Gees CD. Anyone who has ever struggled with a fleck of dust on a CD causing it to skip might well class this particular experiment as coming from the realms of science fiction, rather than science fact.

Although CDs were massive when it came to pop music, with releases such as Dire Straits' 1985 album *Brothers in Arms* forever being associated with the new recording format, they were a real boon for classical music, too. Audiophiles will argue for ever about the merits of vinyl versus CD, but it would be true to say that for many ordinary listeners, their new compact-disc players gave them a far better listening experience than their old record players. And, given the dynamic range of classical music, the CD was infinitely preferable to cassette tapes, where many of the quieter passages of some of the greatest works were almost entirely drowned out by audio hiss. We discuss digital (as opposed to analogue) recordings later in the next moment, but this was also seized on by classical fans as a real benefit.

When sales of CDs started to wane, the record industry attempted to introduce alternative physical formats as a replacement. The thinking went that if they could recreate the explosion of demand that the introduction of CDs brought about, then they could secure their businesses for a few more decades. But the DAT (Digital Audio Tape) and the Minidisc never really caught on for normal consumers, although both products were used extensively by broadcast and recording professionals. It wasn't until downloads began to gain popular support that the CD's days began to look numbered.

NEW WAYS OF DOING BUSINESS: THE BUDGET CLASSICAL LABEL

The story behind the launch of the record label Naxos is one of an entrepreneur who saw a business opportunity and seized it with both hands. Back in the 1970s, the record industry did exactly what its name would suggest – it made records. Good old-fashioned vinyl was the order of the day, along with the infinitely more portable, but far poorer quality, cassette tape.

Record companies were big corporate beasts that tended to span the globe, with the largest labels in Europe including the British classical music powerhouses Decca and EMI, as well as the Hamburg-based Deutsche Grammophon and Philips, which was of Dutch origin. The latter was an offshoot of the company now best known for making televisions, pulsating electric toothbrushes and their distinctive round-headed electric razors. Across the pond, things were already rather more multimedia with two of the biggest labels being owned by the television and radio broadcasters RCA and CBS.

These big labels, known as the 'majors', signed up all of the biggest names in classical music, and no self-respecting conductor, soloist or orchestra was without an exclusive recording contract with one of their number. It gave them a calling card around the world and enabled them to record for posterity their own particular versions of the greatest works in the classical repertoire. Back in those days, the record companies were not averse to splashing the cash when it came to signing up the artists, making recordings of the highest possible quality and promoting their records around the world. That isn't to suggest that these albums were always profitable. Often, it was the pop and rock divisions of the major record labels that were bankrolling each company's classical arm, giving the green light to projects that would ordinarily bring accountants out in a cold sweat. Having a roster of the finest classical artists and creating beautiful classical recordings was seen as a way of enhancing a record company's brand.

In the early 1980s, the compact disc was starting to gain traction (as we discussed in the previous Moment) and it was at this point that Klaus Heymann, a German businessman based in Hong Kong, decided to step into the classical record arena. His business model was simple: he would make new digital recordings of the great classical works and would offer them at a price that would significantly undercut those of the majors. He could do this by making his own recordings, often with far less well-known orchestras and soloists from Eastern Europe who didn't demand telephone-number-sized fees and were grateful for the exposure. He ensured that he owned the rights to the recordings and could exploit them anywhere in the world in any format. Often, he owned the company in each territory that distributed his CDs, thereby ensuring that he wasn't having to pay out to expensive middlemen.

And he thought very differently about where his CDs were sold, too. In 1988, Naxos was the exclusive classical label for Woolworths. Although this store is one of many to have disappeared from our high streets over the past few years, at the time it was a significant player in CD sales, with as many as one in ten discs sold in the UK being rung through its tills. The 'Naxos price' for a CD (around a third of the sum being demanded by the majors) became a major pull for those classical music lovers who were keen to replace their vinyl and cassette recordings with CDs. So, Tchaikovsky's *1812 Overture* and Beethoven's *'Moonlight' Sonata* found themselves sitting alongside Woolworth's infamous pick 'n' mix confectionery and their array of budget-priced household goods. In terms of taking classical music to the masses, Heymann had hit on a sure-fire recipe for business success.

The major record companies did respond by bringing out new lines of their back-catalogue recordings, featuring many of their major star names. But Heymann was able to point out to consumers that his recordings were 100 per cent digital, right through every stage of the recording process. Naxos albums carried the legend 'DDD' on their front cover – **D**igital recording, **D**igital mixing and **D**igital mastering. The older recordings from the majors could only manage 'ADD' on their front covers. They were taking advantage of the latest technology for mixing and mastering the albums, but the original recordings predated digital technology, so they could muster only an 'A' for **A**nalogue recording.

At this point it is important to note that there are many arguments around the sound quality of various recording techniques and, indeed, about the quality of CDs versus vinyl albums, which we have already explored in a little more detail in Moment No. 40. However, it did give Heymann's budget label a real point of difference. Although the critics were sniffy about some of his early recordings made in far-flung parts of Eastern Europe, the record buyers at Woolworths and other high-street stores who wanted to build up a solid classical CD collection efficiently and inexpensively tended not to pay much attention to what the critical elite of hallowed classical music institutions such as *Gramophone* magazine had to say on the subject anyway. It didn't matter to them that they had only a hazy idea of where the cities that housed the orchestras exactly were, let alone any name recognition of the orchestras or performers themselves.

As Naxos grew and the appetite for recording the core classics by major labels began to wane, so the upstart began to pick up more well-known orchestras, conductors and artists. Critical acclaim also followed, with recent recordings such as the Royal Liverpool Philharmonic's series of Shostakovich symphonies under the baton of Vasily Petrenko consistently receiving rave reviews.

When sales of CDs began to drop off with the advent of digital downloads, Heymann once again showed himself to be ahead of the game. Naxos was among the first labels to digitise its entire catalogue, quickly making its recordings available wherever and however digital music was being sold.

ON TOP OF THE WORLD: THE THREE TENORS IN ROME

On 7 July 1990, the three finest tenors in the world at that time performed a concert that will forever be remembered as one of the most important events in the history of classical music. As a result of what happened that evening, The Three Tenors would go on to release the biggest-selling classical album of all time, introducing millions of people to opera and making the men in question household names across the globe.

This particular concert, at the ancient Baths of Caracalla in Rome, had actually been planned at relatively short notice, a little earlier that same year. Luciano Pavarotti and Placido Domingo had agreed to perform with their fellow tenor José Carreras to raise money for the latter's own International Leukemia Foundation, which had been set up following his recovery from the illness. Originally, the whole point of the concert had not been to achieve global stardom or make millions of pounds for the participants; rather, it was primarily a charitable venture designed to reintroduce Carreras to the public consciousness after a period of recuperation that had followed his treatment.

Much of the concert involved each of the tenors taking it in turns to sing a solo item. But, with a few exceptions, it was the occasions when they collaborated as a trio that captured the imagination of the millions of people watching the event across the world. The evening's mixture of operatic arias, Neapolitan songs and Broadway show tunes provided a sure-fire hit – and the inclusion of one particular aria from Puccini's opera *Turandot* ensured that Luciano Pavarotti cemented his position as the world's most famous tenor.

Pavarotti's electrifying version of 'Nessun Dorma' became, in effect, the anthem of Italia '90. The BBC used it for its television coverage of the event and, for many thousands of football fans, it became synonymous with a tournament that, all too predictably, saw England crash out to Germany in the semi-final, after Chris Waddle and Stuart Pearce failed to land their penalties in the back of the net. It was previously unthinkable that opera would feature at the world's largest international football event, but The Three Tenors were an instant hit and became a regular fixture at the World Cup, performing again in 1994, 1998 and 2002. In the immediate aftermath of Italia '90, Pavarotti's version of 'Nessun Dorma' made it to Number 2 in the UK Pop Singles Chart – an astonishing achievement for a piece of classical music.

It's worth remembering that at this point in history, classical music was not a particularly accessible genre for many people in this country – nor for those further afield, too. Classic FM was two years away from launching, so the UK lacked a genuinely populist classical music radio station, and those in control of the TV schedules wouldn't normally have dreamed of putting a large-scale opera or mainstream orchestral concert in a prime-time slot. The World Cup was different, though: The Three Tenors' performance was part and parcel of the opening celebrations, so it was inevitable that it would feature worldwide. What was most definitely not inevitable, though, was that the evening would lead to thousands of people – many of whom had not previously considered classical music to be for them – queuing to buy a recording of a Puccini aria.

Within a couple of years, the live recording of that night's concert had sold over ten million copies, with an additional one million sales on video. From this point onwards, it was abundantly clear to record company executives that they could make a lot of money from classical music. Gone was the preconception from some that this was a niche genre. Instead, The Three Tenors were arguably responsible for inspiring the signing of all sorts of crossover artists in the 1990s, artists deemed to have the same kind of charisma and mass appeal as Pavarotti, Domingo and Carreras.

As for The Three Tenors, they, in effect, became a massive commercial brand themselves. For the rest of the decade, they performed not just at two more World Cups but also in standalone concerts right around the world. In 1996 alone, Pavarotti, Domingo and Carreras sang together in Tokyo, London, Vienna, Vancouver and a whole host of other cities. The format of these concerts was, on one level, very simple: they would always be extremely credible, using a world-class orchestra and an extremely fine conductor. Not for them the accusation that this was classical music done on the cheap. And the music would be accessible, richly melodic and broadly operatic in style. There would be guest performers, too, on occasion, but what the public overwhelmingly wanted to hear was the voices of these three star tenors, who had so won them over when they performed at the start of Italia '90.

The enduring appeal of The Three Tenors was made poignantly evident on the death of Luciano Pavarotti in September 2007. His passing was headline news right around the world – and, once again, his inimitable 'Nessun Dorma' surged into the charts. Although Pavarotti was in many ways the front man of the trio in terms of the publicity he garnered, Domingo and Carreras have also remained hugely popular, not just within the core operatic world they inhabit but among the wider music-loving public, too. Nearly 25 years on from Italia '90, their performance in Rome remains one of the most exciting, groundbreaking and commercially successful moments in the history of classical music – and the legacy of that one night is sure to outlive them all for decades to come.

MUSIC FOR THE MASSES: CLASSIC FM IS BORN

I t might seem a little bit on the arrogant side for us to include the launch of Classic FM in a book of *50 Moments That Rocked the Classical Music World* that is actually published by the radio station itself. But, way back in the introduction, we did say that our selection of significant events was firmly rooted in the world of Classic FM. And during our lengthy debates about what we should and should not include in this book, we felt that it would have been a bit odd to have missed this entry out simply from the point of view of our being rather British and wishing to hide our light under a bushel. So, we have decided to put our bashfulness to one side.

The beginnings of the radio station date back to the early 1990s, when the then government advertised a brand new Independent National Radio licence for a station to broadcast on FM right across the UK. It was a first for commercial radio, where licences up until that point had been available only on a local basis, usually centred around a particular city, or serving a distinct county area. There was one stipulation that the government made: the winning bid must run a non-pop music service. There was much discussion about how exactly to define pop music, with a memorable debate on the subject in the House of Lords.

The licence was initially awarded to a station called 'Showtime', which planned to broadcast the music of West End musical theatre. But the consortium behind the show tunes station didn't manage to get all of its funding in place, so the licence was handed to the next highest bidder and Classic FM was born.

The radio station burst into life at six o'clock in the morning on 7 September 1992, with Nick Bailey hosting the very first breakfast programme. Handel's *'Zadok the Priest'* heralded the start of the new station, which was differenti-ated from the existing classical music station, BBC Radio 3, by its broadcasting of shorter excerpts of classical music favourites through the day, presented by friendly yet know-ledgeable presenters, many of whom were well known from having worked in other areas of the media.

To say that there were some doom-mongers with a pes-simistic view of Classic FM's potential for success back in 1992 would be the understatement of the year. But the naysayers who predicted that the new commercial station, which relied on advertising to pay the bills and received no state subsidy, would speedily fizzle out were proved wrong. Classic FM quickly gained an audience almost three times the size of Radio 3.

So what was the secret of this particular success story? Well, from those earliest days of broadcasting, Classic FM has always believed that classical music can and should be a part of everyone's lives – no matter who they are or where they come from. Today, as part of Global Radio, the UK's leading commercial radio group, the station remains as true to that ideal as it did when it began broadcasting.

Classic FM has been a major supporter of the classical record industry over the last two decades, giving many young classical music performers their first radio airplay. The 'Full Works' record label with Decca is acknowledged to be the most successful of its kind, and the station has been the main media partner of the Classic BRIT Awards since their launch at the start of the new millennium. Classic FM was the first to broadcast a classical chart; the first to allow listeners to phone in on-air to request their favourite classical music; and the first to treat film and videogame soundtracks as a serious part of the classical repertoire. That pioneering spirit can also be seen in the development of a host of new ways of engaging audiences in listening to classical music using the opportunities afforded by technological advances. This is particularly the case with the internet, which was still the preserve of a small academic community when Classic FM launched in 1992.

That desire to share the passion for the music played on-air is another core tenet of Classic FM. When the station first began broadcasting, it soon became clear that some potential listeners found the whole classical world rather daunting. So, Classic FM made it its mission to blast open the doors of classical music, which, at the time, some parts of the artistic elite seemed to believe should remain locked and barred to new listeners. A prime example of how the radio station has challenged this perception is the Classic FM Hall of Fame. Launched in 1996, this annual poll of listeners' classical music tastes remains the largest of its kind anywhere in the world, with Rachmaninov's *Piano Concerto No. 2* the most popular classical work of all time in the aggregated chart.

In the orchestral world, the station has developed deep relationships with orchestras the length and breadth of the country, including the Royal Scottish National Orchestra, Royal Northern Sinfonia, the Royal Liverpool Philharmonic Orchestra, the Orchestra of Opera North, the Philharmonia Orchestra, the London Symphony Orchestra and the Bournemouth Symphony Orchestra. There is nothing quite so thrilling as seeing the whites of the eyes of a group of talented musicians performing truly wonderful music just a few metres in front of you. If you have never tried it, you really should because, make no mistake, you still can't beat hearing live music in the same room as the musicians who are making it. So, more than two decades after its launch, Classic FM's commitment to encouraging people up and down the country to enjoy live classical music in the concert hall remains as strong as ever, just as it does to bringing the world's greatest music to millions of people every day via the radio and the internet.

CLASSICAL – BUT NOT AS YOU KNOW IT: CROSSOVER MUSIC

A quick look at the sales figures of some of the most popular albums in the Classic FM Chart in recent years demonstrates the overwhelming dominance of what is termed 'classical crossover'. From Russell Watson's *The Voice*, which has sold more than 750,000 copies and counting, to Katherine Jenkins, whose albums *Second Nature*, *Serenade* and *Living a Dream* have all sold in excess of half a million units, the releases that break through into the consciousness of the mainstream pop music world are a force to be reckoned with. Classical crossover isn't limited to these light, mass-appeal albums, though – and nor is the phenomenon a recent one. To discover the effect of crossover music on the classical world, we need to wind back to the 1940s.

Seventy years ago, the term 'classical crossover' hadn't yet been coined, but it was most certainly already in existence. As its name would suggest, the phrase relates to music from the classical world that in some way crosses over into the wider public consciousness, rather than being enjoyed only by those people who are the more regular consumers of the classical genre. In the 1940s, the American tenor Mario Lanza set himself on the path to stardom when he signed a deal with MGM Studios in Hollywood. This led to him appearing in a series of popular films – among them *The Great Caruso* and *The Midnight Kiss*. This, in turn, helped Lanza to secure a record deal with the prestigious RCA Red Seal label. Lanza's good looks, warm tenor voice and ease in front of the camera made him a star whose name quickly became known not just in America but across much of the rest of the Western world. The song with which Lanza is most associated, '*Be My Love*' from the film *The Toast of New Orleans*, became his signature tune, selling more than two million copies and making it to the top of America's Billboard chart.

Many would argue that Lanza's achievements in the mainstream were down to his choice of repertoire. Not for him what some regarded as the 'stuffy' classical music of old; instead, he brought his releases to life with all sorts of popular songs and accessible music. The problem is that this argument doesn't necessarily ring true, when you consider that Mario Lanza held the top spot on the Billboard chart with an album comprised entirely of operatic arias, proving that his success was arguably more because of the way in which his recordings were performed, presented and packaged, rather than because he necessarily needed to play down his association with classical music. Many core classical performers since – from James Galway to Luciano Pavarotti – have trodden a similar recording pathway, proving that it's possible to achieve recognition on a wide level while still performing core repertoire in a credible way.

Prior to Mario Lanza, there were other artists who could lay claim to having marked the dawn of classical crossover (the Irish-American singer John McCormack, for example) although none of them achieved anything like the sales figures of the American tenor. As you look at the musicians who have achieved the most in the crossover market since then, a large part of their success has inevitably been down to what marketing types rather irritatingly call their 'unique selling point', or 'USP'. Katherine Jenkins is the girl next door everyone can identify with – the forces' sweetheart whose voice, stage presence and beautiful looks appeal to audiences the world over. Russell Watson is 'The People's Tenor' – a decent British grafter who earned his spurs on the working men's club circuit in the north-west of England and went on to deserved stardom. Hayley Westenra's debut album, *Pure*, is aptly titled: her image and persona are at one with the name of her record.

Not all musicians who are badged with this term are entirely happy with it, though – not least, the man who is often referred to as the 'King of Crossover'. The Italian tenor Andrea Bocelli has been a chart-topper for two decades. His approach led to the term 'popera' being widely used from the mid-1990s onwards, and he now has his own star on the Hollywood Walk of Fame. But Bocelli is wary of some of the ways in which he's described by the music industry. In an interview with the *South China Morning Post*, he once commented, 'Crossover music has a very specific meaning. I do not sing crossover music. When I sing opera I sing opera, and when I sing popular music I sing popular music. Yes, I sing classical arias and popular songs side by side, but never mixed up.'

Not all the artists who are described as being classical crossover material come from the same stable. The best case in point is a spikey-haired, Mockney-accented violinist who, in the early 1990s, broke through the million barrier with his recording of Vivaldi's *Four Seasons*. Nigel Kennedy was definitely not standard crossover material: instead of boyish good looks and a precise centre parting, here was a violinist who seemed to embody rebellion. From his quirky haircut to his unusual choice of clothing, which included an ever present Aston Villa scarf, Kennedy seemed to eschew the Establishment and instead embrace an entirely different image. All the while, though, his playing remained exceptional. Given that he had studied with the great Yehudi Menuhin, this is perhaps unsurprising. Interestingly, Menuhin himself had been a crossover star in his day, thanks in no small part to his jazz-infused album with Stéphane Grappelli.

Classical crossover has embodied many forms over the years: from the fresh young faces of All Angels and Hayley Westenra to the musicians whose presence at a particular moment in history has led them to become household names, such as The Three Tenors. There have also been times when pop stars have got in on the act (Sting's recordings of John Dowland's lute music, for example). Occasionally, the classical artists have gone the other way, with the 2007 release *Andreas Scholl Goes Pop* springing to mind. The latest generation of television talent shows has also led to the creation of new classical crossover artists, with the 'popera' band G4 and the mobile-phone salesman turned international singing star Paul Potts, spawned by *The X Factor* and *Britain's Got Talent*. In nearly all these cases though, their success pales into insignificance when compared to the master. All of the current crop of stars should tip their hats to the trailblazing success of Mario Lanza, who proved to the world that it was possible for a tenor to storm the pop charts.

DIGITAL DEXTERITY: COMPOSING ON COMPUTER

It would be fair to say that most of us are not on first name terms with Emily Howell. And one of the main reasons for this is that Emily is not a person, but a computer. In 2009, 'she' stirred up some controversy after her creator, Professor David Cope, announced his intention to release a CD of Emily's compositions. However, the dawn of composing on computer came not in 2009, but several decades earlier. And it was something that would shake up the classical music world in all sorts of ways.

In the 1950s, a Nebraskan computer programmer by the name of Max Mathews was working at Bell Laboratories in New Jersey. By day, he would develop computer systems for use in the telephone industry, but in his spare time he created a piece of sound-generating software called, appropriately enough, 'MUSIC'. Mathews would use state-of-the-art computers to create sounds that were at first relatively primitive. But by 1958, an updated version of the software ('MUSIC II') was in use. This one made it possible for Mathews's computers to emit polyphonic music – in other words, multiple lines of melody and harmony – and over the years ahead, newer, more ambitious versions of the 'MUSIC' software were created and updated by him.

In the mid-20th century, significant technological advances were being made, as programmers and composers alike experimented with the use of computers in music, with plenty of differing results. One of the most exciting developments in the classical music world came when computers were used to notate these composers' works. This didn't really come to the fore until the 1980s, in tandem with the rise in popularity of the personal computer. It's all too easy to forget that before this time, people simply did not own computers in their homes. The fax machine was still a revelation; letters were written using a typewriter; and musicians would write their music down using good old-fashioned pen and paper.

This didn't remain the case for long, though. The spread of computers in the Western world led to the development of a range of clever music software, which made it quicker and easier to capture composers' ideas. The advent of this score-writing software opened up a whole new range of possibilities. No longer was it necessary to notate every bar of music; instead, composers needed only to connect their computers to an electric keyboard, play in their melodies, and watch as the notes appeared on the screen in front of them.

One of the world's most popular scorewriters is called Sibelius. Along with an American system called Finale, it now jostles to be the most popular piece of music software of its kind in the world. Sibelius was the brainchild of two British twins, Ben and Jonathan Finn, who were both keen musicians. They found the process of writing music down rather tedious and time-consuming, and therefore decided to try to develop a system that did all the legwork for them. The first version of Sibelius was released in 1993, and it rapidly became extremely popular – not just with composers but with educators, too. Not only could this new system be used to notate music electronically, it also enabled composers to listen back to what they had written, without having to enlist the help of a 60-piece symphony orchestra. Rather handy, given that hiring an orchestra is a particularly costly affair.

The development of Sibelius, Finale and other rival versions of score-writing software made it possible for many different people to experiment with composing music. In schools, it was no longer necessary to be able to read music before students could write it. Instead, all they needed to do was to play a melody and the computer would capture every sound that the budding young composers had made. If they then needed to transpose the tune higher or lower, that could be done at the click of a button. Everything was suddenly less arduous and more instinctive.

For composers of large-scale, symphonic music, score-writers were a revelation. Previously, every single part would have had to be carefully written out, and any instruments that weren't in the original key would need to have their parts notated at an alternative pitch. This took an awfully long time, and probably put off many fine musicians from writing a piece of music in the first place. The idea of being hidden away in a room for months, with only a piano, a pencil and a large pile of manuscript paper for company was hardly enticing. By contrast, with its tagline of 'manuscript paper that can think', Sibelius made it possible for composers to focus on the creative aspect of writing music, rather than the laborious task of making a permanent paper record of it.

The development of computer technology over the last half-century has had a major impact on nearly every area of our lives. The effect on the musical world has been substantial. It is now possible for computer programs to compose music, and computers themselves even feature in some concert pieces. But the most groundbreaking and, surely, long-lasting impact of computers is in what they have enabled composers to do. The process of writing music has been opened up to thousands more people through the software created by the Finn brothers and their contemporaries, to the point that many modern-day composers wouldn't dream of attempting their craft without having their computer to hand.

There are some exceptions, though: in an interview with Classic FM in 2012, the legendary film composer John Williams told us he still insists on using his trusty pencil and manuscript paper, and eschews all attempts by others to persuade him to use a computer. And although that might seem a little old-fashioned, with music as wonderful as *Star Wars*, *Schindler's List* and *E.T.*, it's hard to argue that, for some composers, at least, modern technology can still be happily avoided – even in the 21st century.

MUSIC AS PEACE: THE WEST-EASTERN DIVAN ORCHESTRA

Just as the saying goes that you shouldn't work with children or animals, some people firmly adhere to the view that music and politics should never mix. And yet, there have been many examples through the years of musicians and politicians coming together to do good or to effect a major change for the better. In pop music, Bob Geldof's and Midge Ure's exhortation to 'Feed the World' and their championing of the Live Aid project brought the plight of the millions of people starving in Africa to the top of the in-trays of presidents and prime ministers around the globe in the 1980s.

In classical music, there is no better example of the power of the art form to raise the profile of an issue and to create debate than the creation of the West-Eastern Divan Orchestra. It all started back in 1999 and was the brain-child of the Argentine-Israeli pianist and conductor Daniel Barenboim and the Palestinian literary scholar Edward Said.

The two men, whose nationalities bridged the religious divide that has been at the centre of conflict in the Middle East for decades, were asked to put together a workshop for young people from Israel, Palestine and other Arab countries in the region. Their objectives were twofold: first, they wanted to open up a dialogue between the young people from the two distinct faith groups; and, second, they wanted to get them working together at something that they all enjoyed doing. At its simplest, what the two founders wanted was the participants to talk to each other and to play music together. Both activities involve listening.

The project's name derives from a series of poems penned by the 18th- and 19th-century German writer Johann Wolfgang von Goethe, called *West-Eastern Divan*. Written between 1814 and 1819 and then expanded in 1827, this is not poetry for the faint-hearted, running as it does to twelve books. At its core is the idea of propagating the healthy exchange between the Orient (the Eastern world) and the Occident (the Western world).

The first time the West-Eastern Divan Orchestra came together was more than a decade ago in Weimar, with a follow-up session taking place in Chicago. By 2002, it had gained a permanent residence in the Spanish city of Seville, which has been its home ever since. It's an expensive business running any symphony orchestra and this is especially the case when you consider that the young musicians are drawn from countries across the Middle East. It means that the orchestra relies on the fundraising efforts of a series of charitable foundations to ensure that it is able to carry out its work.

So what drove a musician like Daniel Barenboim to become involved in the first place? His pedigree as one of the all-time classical music greats is unquestionable, with music directorships of La Scala in Milan, the Berlin State Opera, the Chicago Symphony Orchestra and the Orchestre de Paris under his belt. As a pianist, he has played with nearly all of the world's greatest orchestras in virtually all of the world's most significant concert halls. He is known to many classical music lovers as the former husband of the brilliant British cellist Jacqueline du Pré, who was struck down by multiple sclerosis while in the prime of her career.

Alongside his life as a performer, Barenboim has a long history of being politically vocal and active. However, he has been very clear in saying that he does not believe that the orchestra in itself is a 'project for peace'. Rather, he argues that it is a 'project against ignorance'. Along with Edward Said, who died of leukemia in 2003, he believed that by playing alongside each other in an orchestral setting, young Israeli and Arab people would gain a greater comprehension of each other's point of view. At the end of each period working together, they might still hold opposing opinions, so in Barenboim's words, 'the Divan is not a love story'. However, he hopes that each time the orchestra plays he has managed to 'create a platform where the two sides can disagree and not resort to knives'. Edward Said and Daniel Barenboim expanded on their thinking in this area in a series of public talks they held on the subject at Carnegie Hall in New York. Eventually, these were turned into a well-received book *Parallels and Paradoxes: Exploration in Music and Society.*

Unsurprisingly, with Barenboim as its chief conductor, the standard of playing by the orchestra is extremely high and it has toured around the world to great critical acclaim. In London, the orchestra's performance of all nine of Beethoven's symphonies in the 2012 Proms season was hailed as an enormous success. It was the first time that the whole cycle had been performed in one season at the Royal Albert Hall since the mighty undertaking had been carried out with aplomb by the festival's founder Henry Wood some 70 years earlier in 1942.

Those who run the orchestra believe that a military resolution of the Middle East conflict is an unlikely outcome and that whatever happens in the future, the peoples on both sides of the conflict will be linked together, not least by geography. So the success of this orchestra and the reason for including it as one of our 50 moments is not because its creation has instantaneously delivered world peace. Rather, we have included it in our list because its existence offers a model for how a generation of talented young performers from different backgrounds can come together for the first time, regarding each other as equals, recognising each other's talent and listening to each other play and talk. It's Daniel Barenboim's belief that this act of listening will, in the long term, help to engender a greater understanding from all sides in a particularly troubled area of the world. And if classical music can play its part in making that happen, that feels like a positive step forward.

THE NEXT GENERATION: THE SIMÓN BOLÍVAR YOUTH ORCHESTRA AND EL SISTEMA

Although there is an amazing amount of brilliant music-making that goes on among young people the world over, hear the words 'children performing' and it's very easy to conjure up in your mind's eye a picture of a cold school concert hall echoing to the sounds of screechy violins and mistimed cymbal crashes. Actually, we think that this caricature is pretty unfair, but it does still persist. Every year when we judge the Classic FM Music Teacher of the Year competition, we get to see and hear some jaw-droppingly good performances from school orchestras. And then there's the National Children's Orchestra (for pre-teens) and the National Youth Orchestra, which showcases the UK's finest teenage classical music talent.

So let's be absolutely clear: just because we've chosen to write about an orchestra that was born in Venezuela and has become famous right around the globe, we don't for a moment think that our own home-grown young musicians are in any way second class when compared to their South American cousins. You have only to join us on our annual pilgrimage to the Music for Youth Schools Prom at London's Royal Albert Hall to hear just how musically talented British schoolkids really are. It's just that this particular youth orchestra from Venezuela has captured the imagination of concert-goers in a way that no other orchestra made up of young people quite seems to have managed. The reason? Well, they are undoubtedly great musicians who know how to put on a spectacular musical show. But, they also have a great story to tell. And it's this story that has helped ensure that audiences take them to their hearts wherever they perform.

The tale began back in 1975, when a Venezuelan economist called José Antonio Abreu founded a music education programme in his native land, with the aim of creating a national network of orchestras for young people across the country. It became known as 'El Sistema' and four decades later has grown to a web of 125 separate, but affiliated, orchestras. More than 300,000 children take part in the programme, with the vast majority coming from economically deprived backgrounds.

The philosophy behind El Sistema sees the symphony orchestra as a metaphor for the stable family unit that many of these children simply don't enjoy. There is little doubt that Abreu, who has been much lauded for his work in this area, is something of a visionary. He has also shown considerable skill in ensuring that the Venezuelan government of the day, no matter what its political make-up, has continued to back the project. In some ways, the heart of El Sistema isn't really about music at all: it's a high-impact social-action project that uses music as a tool to change young people's lives. It instils discipline, teaches camaraderie, improves the ability to learn by rote, gives young people a sense of belonging, widens employment prospects and allows the young musicians to gain a sense of the world outside the tough streets from where they come. At the same time, it takes all of them on a journey through music. And the very best of them become astoundingly accomplished musicians. So, even if the project's aim is more about changing communities and young lives for the better, proficiency in music is unquestionably a by-product. José Antonio Abreu has himself recognised the complex relationship between the music itself and its ability to effect change, describing it as 'an agent of social development'.

The most famous of all of these Venezuelan orchestras is the Simón Bolívar Youth Orchestra, which first came to prominence in the UK and USA in 2007 under the baton of the inspirational young conductor Gustavo Dudamel. With his engaging personality, energetic conducting style and wild mop of black hair, he quickly became a charismatic figure in the world of classical music. He is known to many as 'The Dude', and it was unsurprising that the Los Angeles Philharmonic came calling and appointed him their Principal Conductor. There can be few individuals who are credible classical music performers and have big enough personalities to stand out in Tinseltown. It's testament to Dudamel's magnetic charm that he has appeared in a television advertisement for California alongside Governor Arnold Schwarzenegger.

The Simón Bolívar Youth Orchestra has recorded with Dudamel on the Deutsche Grammophon label, specialising in Latin American classical music alongside more core works from the Western classical tradition. Its sound is big and bold and its performances crackle with vibrant energy – unsurprising really, when you consider that the orchestra is twice the size of the standard symphony outfit.

Music educators around the world have been impressed by the clear benefits of El Sistema on communities in Venezuela and they have set about creating their own variations of the project, which sees young people submerged in music-making, usually on a daily basis. The music director of the Berlin Philharmonic, Simon Rattle, has described El Sistema as 'nothing less than a miracle . . . From here, I see the future of music for the whole world.'

In Scotland, the former Bishop of Edinburgh, Richard Holloway, set up The Big Noise as a means of helping to regenerate Raploch in Stirlingshire, with backing from the Scottish Arts Council. The violinist Nicola Benedetti is among the scheme's many leading supporters. While in England, the Department for Education and Arts Council England now jointly fund six In Harmony programmes in Leeds, Liverpool, Newcastle and Gateshead, Nottingham, Telford and Stoke-on-Trent and the London borough of Lambeth. Support for the English programme has been spearheaded by the cellist Julian Lloyd Webber.

The arguments in favour of the Scottish and English projects are compelling, with hard data showing an increase in levels of attainment at school among the young participants, along with huge amounts of anecdotal evidence suggesting that the introduction of classical music learning and performance into these young people's lives is changing the entire environment in which they find themselves living. Many of the critics of the British schemes felt that teaching young people about classical music was too elitist and would simply never work. But try telling that to the kids, who are tutored by players from the Royal Liverpool Philharmonic Orchestra, at the In Harmony scheme in West Everton. For them, classical music has become an unremarkable part of their everyday lives – in itself, a truly remarkable feat.

TECHNOLOGY CHANGES EVERYTHING AGAIN: THE DIGITAL DOWNLOAD REVOLUTION

Some of our *50 Moments That Rocked the Classical Music World* have happened relatively recently, while others took place a considerable amount of time in the past. This particular moment is important because we are living in the middle of it right now. Perhaps some people might argue that we should wait to see if history judges it as being truly significant, but when we discussed what to include and what to leave out of this book, we were in complete agreement that this moment is massive for classical music, although we are still only just beginning to see its effects. Having said that, the pace of technological change is now so quick that by the time this book is just a few years old, we believe that digital downloading will be the most significant way in which people buy classical music.

Recorded music itself and the way in which it is

distributed is something that we have come back to time and time again in this book. Whether it was the invention of the printing press, the wax cylinder, the gramophone or the CD, the fortunes of the people who write and perform music are intrinsically linked to the success of its distribution.

Much has been written about the music industry's slowness in responding to the tsunami of digital music available online. Much of it is available illegally free of charge, thus robbing composers and performers of the royalties that are rightfully theirs for creating the music in the first place. Initially, MP3 files were sold legally on sites such as Napster, but when Apple's first iPod was released, everything changed. This was a desirable piece of kit with five or ten gigabytes of storage capacity, allowing the equivalent of more than two thousand pop songs to be stored.

The CD may not yet be dead, but even the most ardent compact-disc fan concedes that its share of the overall recorded music market is in sharp decline, with digital distribution now in rapid growth, thanks in the main to the success of Apple and its iPods, iPhones and iPads, which are filled with music bought digitally from its online iTunes store. The beauty of iTunes and other download stores is their ability to satisfy immediately the musical desires of even the most adventurous music enthusiast.

For classical music fans, iTunes offers the opportunity to be able to browse through thousands of different titles, as well as being able to sample snippets before having to hand over any cash. True, it can be a little daunting to try to navigate through the hundreds of different versions of popular works, but the software behind the store helps direct users to the bestselling versions of works first. That, combined with a performer, orchestra or record label whose name you recognise, makes it easier to make a better-informed choice.

Not only has the number of record shops on our high streets rapidly declined over the past few years, but the space given over to classical music has also dwindled. That means that online stores really do allow the listener more easily to unearth rarer recordings, or those made by smaller specialist labels. Many of our great symphony orchestras are issuing their work on their own labels. The London Symphony Orchestra's *LSO Live* label is a great success; while Harry Christophers' choir The Sixteen releases much of its work on its own Coro label; and the conductor John Eliot Gardiner has a very successful series of beautifully packaged albums on his SDG label. Smaller labels such as Avie have sprung up offering recordings of well-established artists who now no longer work exclusively with one major record company. All of these labels sell their albums via iTunes, giving them an exposure to potential purchasers that they could only have dreamed of in all but the most specialist record stores. Completely new names have also begun to have success in the classical sphere alongside the established big-name record labels such as Decca, Deutsche Grammophon, EMI, Sony and Warner Music. Take X5, for example, a Stockholm-based label that launched only in 2003. Just seven years later, it was the bestselling classical label in the American Billboard charts, through digital releases alone.

Of course, other download sites do exist, with Amazon offering its own service of MP3 downloads and some of the smaller classical labels, such as the excellent Hyperion and Chandos, offering a bespoke download service of their own material on their websites. There are also smaller aggregation services that sell music released on a range of different classical labels. Only time will tell whether there is a long-term sustainable business model against the might of Apple's twin-track approach of providing desirable hardware coupled with an impressive online retail store. Just to add to the possibilities, companies such as Spotify and Pandora allow listeners to curate the music they hear in another way altogether, by paying for a streaming service of tracks that they never actually own.

Classical enthusiasts might well have held onto CDs as their method of choice for listening to their music for longer than their pop, rock and dance brethren, but the march of the download towards supremacy now looks unstoppable. And it's easy to see why. The potential to have your entire music collection in good quality in your pocket wherever you go; the chance to listen to it on headphones or transmit it wirelessly to speakers in your home, and the ability to buy a copy of whatever you want to hear at that precise moment in time, wherever you might be, adds up to such a seductive package that it's a surprise only that the dam hasn't been breached before now. One thing is for certain, though: this particular moment of opportunity is rocking the classical music world right now.

WORLD WIDE WEB:
ERIC WHITACRE'S VIRTUAL CHOIR

As we have just described, the internet offers a whole new dimension to the world of classical music. This particular moment isn't about simply commoditising classical music in terms of making a purchase; rather this is more about the creation of an epic online event, allowing people all over the globe to come together to share the *making* of classical music.

It was the brainchild of the American composer Eric Whitacre, whom the *Daily Telegraph* described as being 'that rare thing, a modern composer who is both popular and original'. Now, it would be true to say that many of the finest protagonists in the classical music world over the years have been no oil paintings. And we're not just talking about the brass section of the average symphony orchestra. Many of the greatest composers throughout classical music history have been more than a little lacking in the beautiful-physiognomy department, so you can imagine the excitement levels in dusty classical music circles when their eyes fell on the film-star good looks of the forty-something Nevada-born tunesmith Eric Whitacre.

In fact, with his flowing blond locks and Hollywood-white smile, Whitacre is almost too good to be true for the classical music world. Not only is he so devilishly handsome that he has been signed up by the Storm Model Agency (which also has such lovelies as Carla Bruni, Eva Herzigová and Lily Cole on its books) but he also composes serious contemporary classical music really rather well. And even more than that, it's serious contemporary classical music that has built him a massive fanbase right around the world. Whitacre's journey towards international stardom has been all the more speedy due to his very clever use of the internet and his acute under-standing that, at its best, the world wide web is all about finding ways to build a creative and dynamic community, based on a shared interest. Whereas other composers merely download their music to listeners, Whitacre has harnessed the internet's ability to allow listeners to upload versions of that music to the composer himself, so that it can in turn be downloaded by other listeners. It really is a web in the proper sense of the word.

Before he hit on his brilliant idea, Whitacre began his formal music training at the University of Nevada. He was particularly struck by the music of Mozart – and his *Requiem* in particular. He went on to study composition at the Juilliard School, regarded by many as the USA's pre-eminent perform-ing arts academy. He first came to prominence in the minds of British audiences with the release of his album *Cloudburst* on the Hyperion label. This all-choral disc features performances from the choir Polyphony, conducted by Stephen Layton. It includes the eponymous hit written when Whitacre was just 22 years old, as well as *Lux Aurumque* and *Sleep*.

His first album as both a composer and conductor was entitled *Light and Gold* and was released by Decca Records in 2010. It won a Grammy Award and shot to the top of the classical charts in both the UK and USA. He made easy work of the traditionally 'difficult second album', with his follow-up release for Decca, *Water Night*, topping both the iTunes and Billboard classical charts on the day of release. Performances here were from his newly assembled professional choir, the Eric Whitacre Singers.

So, you might be asking yourself why Whitacre finds his way into the pages of this book. He is a commercially and critically successful composer, but there are plenty of those. True, he's on the books of a model agency and has lectured at universities around the world, to the United Nations and at the infamous TED Conference in Long Beach, California. He has also been the first Composer in Residence at Sidney Sussex College at the University of Cambridge. Impressive as each of these achievements are, none of them has come anywhere close to matching his innovative 'Virtual Choir' project in terms of taking classical music out to new audiences.

A performance of *Lux Aurumque* received over a million views on YouTube in just two months. The secret of its success? It featured 185 singers from 12 different countries, all of whom had uploaded their performance of Whitacre's music, which was then expertly mixed together to create a stunning online audio-visual performance. 'Virtual Choir 2.0' swiftly followed. This time, 2,052 singers from 58 countries performed *Sleep*. In its third incarnation, 'Virtual Choir 3' saw 3,746 singers from 73 countries taking part in a performance of *Water Night*. At the time of writing, the first three Virtual Choir projects have been watched more than 5.5 million times on YouTube alone.

Assembling the videos into one work and building the internet site necessary to make the choirs happen is an expensive business and Whitacre has funded the creation of 'Virtual Choir 4' by asking fans to pledge cash online through Kickstarter, which enables them to pledge relatively small amounts of money, which collectively fund the project. In many ways, this method of raising the readies takes the arts patronage that would have been familiar to many of the great composers of times gone by into a 21st-century digital setting.

The secrets of Whitacre's success are manifold. First – and it's important not to forget this – he writes really good, high-quality music. Choirs want to sing it and audiences want to listen to it. He is a great communicator about music in general – and about his own music in particular. During his concerts, he turns around, faces the audience and tells them in a compelling, succinct way about how each piece came into being. Listeners love to be able to contextualise a work and knowing something of its history allows them to reap greater benefits from what they hear. Finally, he has been a visionary in the way in which he has used new technology to involve listeners in his music on their terms, rather than on his. Whitacre is the antithesis of those who see classical music as a museum piece that can't be relevant to the listeners of today.

COULD VIDEO KILL
THE CLASSICAL STAR?
VIDEOGAME SOUNDTRACKS

O ur fiftieth choice in our *50 Moments That Rocked the Classical Music World* is a controversial one. Having read this far, you may find that hardly surprising. But the difference between this particular musical contretemps and all the others we've written about is that this one is happening right now – and hasn't quite yet resolved itself one way or the other.

In case you aren't completely au fait with the world of gaming, then we will pause for just a minute to explain. There has been an explosion of video games produced for consoles such as the Nintendo Xbox and the Sony PlayStation. Many of these games include especially commissioned classical orchestral soundtracks, written by composers who tend to specialise in the genre. The music is composed so that it develops as a player moves through the game. Structurally, many of the ideas are common to other musical forms, so a composer might use a particular theme to accompany action from a certain character. In terms of the sound-world it inhabits, much of this music features the instruments of a traditional symphony orchestra and we would recognise it as being classical music in its style – so, no pounding rock rhythms, disco beats, or cheesy snare-drum accompaniment to orchestral settings. In many ways, the way it sounds is not dissimilar to the most successful symphonic film soundtracks.

As we described earlier, in Moment No. 28, many classical music performers, listeners and commentators now regard film soundtracks as a legitimate part of the overall canon of classical music repertoire – although, it should be said, some people do feel that the genre should be kept separate from the more core compositions, locked away in its own separate room, if you like.

However, not everyone feels quite so positive about soundtracks that have been written for use on videogames. We found this out for ourselves when, in 2012, we included votes for videogame soundtracks in the Classic FM Hall of Fame, our annual poll of listeners' favourite classical works. By 2013, Nobuo Uematsu's music for the *Final Fantasy* series occupied the No. 3 position in the chart, while Jeremy Soule's *The Elder Scrolls* soundtrack was at No. 5.

Some of our listeners felt that we were wrong to include music that was composed primarily for use on games consoles, arguing that this wasn't classical music. Other people – most notably those involved in the very active gaming community – were delighted that the music they know and love was being accorded artistic status in its own right. Many listeners who didn't have a strong ideological objection to the concept of videogame music being broadcast on a classical music radio station made their judgement on the music itself regardless of its origins – they either liked it, or they didn't.

For our part, we tend to fall in this third category. Just as with every other form of music, whether it be classical or rock, pop, dance or jazz, in the genre of videogame soundtracks, there are good compositions and bad ones, excellent recordings and poor ones, gripping performances and mediocre ones. So, we don't think that all videogame music hits the spot; but there are undoubtedly some very strong compositions that we are delighted to feature as part of Classic FM's extensive playlist.

After all, the composers who are writing this music are following in a long tradition of producing new work to match all of the available means of distribution of the day. We made this argument in Moment No. 28, on film soundtracks, and the case can be made just as forcefully here. The only difference is that film soundtracks have been around for more than a century, but videogame music is a much newer art form – and perhaps one with which many classical music enthusiasts have yet to become familiar.

Unsurprisingly, given the importance of the country in the development of videogame hardware, Japan led the way in recognising that these soundtracks could be sold as musical works in their own right, away from the game environment. In the UK, the London Philharmonic Orchestra has had huge success with two albums of orchestrations of videogame soundtracks conducted by Andrew Skeet. As well as the more recent recordings, these albums include relatively vintage examples of the genre, such as *Sonic the Hedgehog* and *Super Metroid.*

Both the London Symphony Orchestra and the Royal Scottish National Orchestra have enjoyed huge success in presenting live concerts of videogame music, with full symphony orchestras performing the works as traditional classical concerts in their normal concert hall homes. The Philharmonia Orchestra has developed something of a speciality of recording soundtracks for the games, working with leading composers in the field such as Mark Griskey, James Hannigan, Russell Shaw and Christopher Lennertz on titles as wide-ranging as *Harry Potter*, *The Lord of the Rings* and *Command & Conquer.* Indeed, leading videogames companies such as EA Games are now among the more significant commissioners of newly composed symphonic music for orchestras such as the Philharmonia to record today.

And the gradual blending of videogame music into the classical music world isn't limited to the orchestral sector here in the UK. The Czech National Symphony Orchestra has presented videogame music concerts at the Gewandhaus concert hall in Leipzig; the LA Philharmonic played in the first official *Final Fantasy* concert at the Walt Disney Concert Hall in Los Angeles; and the Malmö Symphonic Orchestra has promoted live concerts featuring music from the world of videogames in Sweden. And these examples are just the tip of the iceberg. Without doubt, this is one of the fastest-growing – and fastest-selling – areas of live classical music for the orchestral sector today.

One of the more creatively interesting areas of working with computers is the vast array of possibilities that it opens up for collaboration across art forms. Students at Virginia Tech University in the USA have already seized this opportunity, composing an opera based on the highly successful videogame *Minecraft* and the music of Mozart. They have called the new work *OperaCraft*.

No doubt the debate will continue to rage, but we are more than happy to include it in this book because we believe that this is an area of classical music that will rapidly develop over the next few years. It's another technological advance that will bring with it innovation and opportunity. Welcoming videogame music into the classical fold is certainly controversial, but is it really so different from Moment No. 27, when the premiere of Stravinsky's *The Rite of Spring* caused a riot in Paris? At least, on this occasion, we hope that any violence will be limited to the virtual world, rather than forcing us all to witness fisticuffs in the concert hall.

WHERE TO FIND OUT MORE

If this book has whetted your appetite to find out more, one of the best ways to discover what you like about classical music is to tune in to Classic FM. We broadcast 24 hours a day across the UK on 100–102 FM, on DAB digital radio, online at www.ClassicFM.com, on Sky Channel 0106, on Virgin Media channel 922 and on FreeSat channel 722, or direct to your mobile phone or tablet via our free Android and IOS apps. We play a huge breadth of different classical music each week, so you will be able to start your voyage of discovery simply by tuning in.

As well as being able to listen online, you will find a host of interactive features about classical music, composers and musicians on our website: ClassicFM.com. When we first turned on Classic FM's transmitters more than 20 years ago, we changed the face of classical music radio in the UK for ever. Two decades later, we are doing the same online. So, we've packed our website with up-to-the-minute classical music news, details of the latest recordings and upcoming concerts, big-name interviews and lots of information for anyone who wants to make a personal journey through the world of classical music.

If books are more your thing than websites, then we would very much like to recommend the three companion volumes to *50 Moments That Rocked the Classical Music World*, all of which are published by Elliott & Thompson. We pack more than a thousand years of the world's greatest music into *Everything You Ever Wanted To Know About Classical Music . . . But Were Too Afraid To Ask*, enabling the reader to trace the history of classical music from its birth through to the present day, finding out about all the major composers along the way. We also answer some of the most frequently asked questions about music terms, going to live classical concerts and putting together your own collection of recordings. The second of our companion books is *Classic Ephemera,* a musical miscellany, packed with all manner of handy information: telling trivia, curious quotes and fascinating facts. Finally, *The Classic FM Hall of Fame* profiles the 300 greatest classical works and their composers – as voted by Classic FM listeners.

If you would like to delve far, far deeper into the subject than we have been able to do in this short book, the universally acknowledged authority on the subject is *The New Grove Dictionary of Music and Musicians*. The original version was edited by George Grove, with the eminent musicologist Stanley Sadie for this new edition (published in 1995). But be warned – this is a weighty tome, running to 20 hardback volumes with around 29,000 separate articles.

In truth, this massive resource is far more detailed than most music lovers would ever need; a more manageable reference book is *The Concise Oxford Dictionary of Music*, edited by Michael Kennedy (published by Oxford Reference), or *The Penguin Companion to Classical Music*, edited by Paul Griffiths (published by Penguin). Paul Griffiths has also written *A Concise History of Western Music* (published by Cambridge University Press) – a highly readable discussion of the way in which classical music has evolved over time.

The DK Eyewitness Companion to Classical Music, edited by John Burrows (published by Dorling Kindersley), is a very colourful and reliable source of information on the chronology of classical music. Howard Goodall delves into five episodes that changed musical history, including the invention of musical notation and the creation of the recording industry, in his excellent book *Big Bangs* (published by Vintage). Howard also places classical music in the context of the whole of music history in his highly recommended book *The Story of Music* (published by Chatto & Windus). For a slightly quirkier walk through the subject, we would suggest *Stephen Fry's Incomplete & Utter History of Classical Music*, which is published by Macmillan and is based on the award-winning Classic FM radio series of the same name, written by our breakfast show host Tim Lihoreau.

Other excellent general guides to classical music include: *The Rough Guide to Classical Music*, edited by Joe Staines (published by Rough Guides); *The Encyclopedia of Music* by Max Wade-Matthews and Wendy Thompson (published by Hermes House); *Good Music Guide* by Neville Garden (published by Columbia Marketing); *The Chronicle of Classical Music* by Alan Kendall (published by Thames & Hudson); *The Lives & Times of the Great Composers* by Michael Steen (published by Icon); *The Lives of the Great Composers* by Harold C. Schonberg (published by Abacus); and *Music for the People: The Pleasures and Pitfalls of Classical Music* by Gareth Malone, whose television series on singing are fast making him a national treasure (published by Collins).

Three excellent books on the subject of opera are *The DK Eyewitness Guide to Opera* (published by Dorling Kindersley); *The Good Opera Guide* by Denis Forman (published by Phoenix); and *The Rough Guide to Opera* by Matthew Boyden (published by Rough Guides).

For younger classical music lovers or discoverers, *The Story of Classical Music* and *Famous Composers* are both published by Naxos Audiobooks. These titles, read by the Classic FM presenter Aled Jones, are aimed at eight- to fourteen-year-olds and contain musical excerpts and CD-ROM elements.

The very best way of finding out more about which pieces of classical music you like is by going out and hearing a live performance for yourself. Classic FM has a series of partnerships with orchestras across the country: the Royal Scottish National Orchestra, Royal Northern Sinfonia, the Royal Liverpool Philharmonic Orchestra, the Orchestra of Opera North, the Philharmonia Orchestra, Welsh National Opera Orchestra, the London Symphony Orchestra and the Bournemouth Symphony Orchestra. To see if they have a concert coming up near you, log onto our website at ClassicFM.com and click on the 'Concerts and Events' section. It will also include many of the other classical concerts – both professional and amateur – that are taking place near to where you live.

ACKNOWLEDGEMENTS

No book like this happens without lots of help along the way from the people with whom we work every day at Classic FM. So we want to say a very big 'thank you' to Nick Bailey, Jamie Beesley, Catherine Bott, Alex Brooksbank, John Brunning, Stuart Campbell, Lucy Chisholm-Batten, Alistair Cockburn, Lucy Coward, Jamie Crick, Howard Goodall, Charlotte Green, Alex James, Aled Jones, Bob Jones, Jane Jones, Will Kisby, Myleene Klass, Tim Lihoreau, Laurence Llewelyn-Bowen, Kyle Macdonald, David Mellor, Anne-Marie Minhall, Jenny Nelson, Phil Noyce, Bill Overton, Nicholas Owen, Clare Patterson, Alexandra Philpotts, Sam Pittis, Dan Ross, Mel Spencer, John Suchet, Margherita Taylor, Alan Titchmarsh and Rob Weinberg. Special thanks must go to Emma Oxborrow for her gentle yet forceful encouragement to get the book actually written.

We are also greatly indebted to Global Radio's Founder and Executive President, Ashley Tabor; to Group Chief Executive, Stephen Miron; to Director of Broadcasting,

Richard Park; to Chairman, Lord Allen of Kensington CBE, and to Group Strategy and Development Director, Will Harding. Thanks also to Global's Caeshia St Paul, Giles Pearman, Andrea Flamini, Laxmi Hariharan, John Chittenden and Damaris Brown.

As always, we are incredibly grateful to Lorne Forsyth, Olivia Bays, Jennie Condell, Pippa Crane, Alison Menzies and Thomas Ogilvie at our publishers Elliott & Thompson for guiding us through the process of getting this book into print with their customary enthusiasm, good humour and especially, on this occasion, patience. Excellent publishers are hard to find and they are the finest examples of the species.

ABOUT THE AUTHORS

Darren Henley is the Managing Director of Global Radio's national classical music station, Classic FM. The author of two independent government reviews into music and cultural education and 24 books about classical music and musicians, he chairs the government's Cultural Education Board and the Mayor of London's Music Education Advisory Group. He sits on the University of Warwick Commission on the Future of Cultural Value and is a member of the governing body of the Associated Board of the Royal Schools of Music and a Vice President of the Canterbury Festival. Darren studied Politics at the University of Hull. He is a Fellow of the Royal Society of Arts, of the Radio Academy and of the London College of Music; an Honorary Fellow of Canterbury Christ Church University and of Trinity Laban Conservatoire of Music and Dance; an Honorary Member of the Royal Northern College of Music and of the Incorporated Society of Musicians; and a Companion of the Chartered Management Institute. He has picked up four gold Radio Academy Awards, four Arqiva

Commercial Radio Awards, a Royal Philharmonic Society Award and a Classic BRIT Award. In 2012, he was awarded the Charles Groves Prize for 'his outstanding contribution to British music'. He was appointed an OBE in the 2013 New Year Honours for services to music.

Sam Jackson is the Managing Editor of Classic FM, responsible for all of the station's on-air programming and music output, a role he has held since 2011. In his ten years at Classic FM, his programmes have been honoured by the Sony Radio Academy Awards, the Arqiva Commercial Radio Awards and the New York International Radio Festival. He was chosen as one of the Radio Academy's '30 Under 30' for two consecutive years and in 2012, he was the only person working in radio to be included in *Music Week*'s '30 under 30'. In 2013, the Hospital Club named him as one of 'the 100 most influential, innovative and interesting individuals in the media and creative industries'. A proficient pianist and clarinettist, Sam holds a first-class degree in Music from the University of York. He sits on the governing body of Trinity Laban Conservatoire of Music and Dance and on the University of York Music Department's advisory board, as well as being a trustee of the Radio Academy. The author of two *Sunday Times* bestselling books about classical music, his new book about bringing up young children, *Diary of a Desperate Dad*, is published by Elliott & Thompson. Previously, he enjoyed a career in front of the microphone, as a presenter on the children's digital radio station, Fun Kids.

INDEX

INDEX

INDEX